To those children today who will become
politicians tomorrow. A.C.

First published in Great Britain in 2024 by Red Shed, part of Farshore

An imprint of HarperCollins*Publishers*
1 London Bridge Street, London SE1 9GF
www.farshore.co.uk

HarperCollins*Publishers*
Macken House, 39/40 Mayor Street Upper
Dublin 1, D01 C9W8

Red Shed is a registered trademark of HarperCollins*Publishers* Ltd.

With thanks to Sir Keir Starmer, Rory Stewart, Sir Lindsay Hoyle,
Keira Knightley, Dame Eliza Manningham-Buller, Sadiq Khan, Mete Coban,
Gus O'Donnell, Annabelle Fox, Sarah Hunt and Emma Dods.

ISBN 978 0 00 866612 5
Signed edition ISBN 978 0 00 872186 2
Printed and bound in the UK using 100% Renewable Electricity at CPI Group (UK) Ltd.
001

A CIP catalogue record for this title is available from the British Library.

ALASTAIR CAMPBELL

TALKS

POLITICS

RED
SHED

CONTENTS

INTRODUCTION

'I have a dream . . .' – the most famous line in perhaps the most famous political speech ever made. Even if most people (me included) cannot recite the rest of the speech, most people know that Martin Luther King Jr spoke those words, and we know the central role he played in making the dream come true, as Black Americans finally won civil rights, including the precious right to vote.

Martin Luther King Jr gave his life to his cause, assassinated aged just 39 by a racist murderer determined he shouldn't succeed. I was 11 years old, and his death is one of my earliest political memories. Barack Obama was not even born, yet when he was elected America's first Black President in 2008, he acknowledged the role Martin Luther King Jr and various Civil Rights activists played in getting him there. And King's memory is celebrated in the US every year with a national holiday. Legacy!

I didn't have the same experiences as King. But his speech inspired me to dream about how I wanted to be part of making the world a better place.

I want this book to play a part in firing you up to appreciate why politics matters, the differences for good and bad that it can make, why it can be fun . . . and above all, why it affects us all – whether we realise it or not.

To get this country's politics in better shape, you will need to play a part. That means, at a minimum, being interested. Better still, being engaged and involved. Best of all, thinking about whether the political path might be one that YOU want to take. I hope this book helps you understand what that might mean, and why it matters.

In fact, I hope that one day in the future, the person who is then Prime Minister of the UK posts a photo of a dog-eared copy of this book on an app that does not yet exist, with the comment: 'This is the book that inspired me to get into politics.' Why not? Someone must be Prime Minister and I am telling you . . . whoever you are, wherever you live, whatever your background, maybe it could be you.

ARE YOU READY TO TALK POLITICS?

'POLITICS ARE TOO SERIOUS A MATTER
TO BE LEFT TO THE POLITICIANS.'

CHARLES DE GAULLE, FORMER PRESIDENT
OF FRANCE, RESPONDING TO
FORMER BRITISH PRIME MINISTER
CLEMENT ATTLEE'S OBSERVATION THAT
'DE GAULLE IS A VERY GOOD SOLDIER
AND A VERY BAD POLITICIAN'.

CHAPTER 1

POLITICS MATTERS

WHAT IS POLITICS?

Politics means different things to different people. I covered politics as a journalist for a decade, then worked in politics on the frontline for another decade as spokesman and strategist for Tony Blair, who was **Prime Minister** between 1997 and 2007. I have never stood to be an elected politician myself – the time was never right, either because I was doing another job in politics at that moment, or because of other pressures in my life. But I have done a mix of politics and media ever since, and the way I define politics is:

> **POLITICS IS HOW PEOPLE AND COMMUNITIES MAKE THE DECISIONS THAT AFFECT THE ISSUES OF CONCERN TO THEM.**

That is a broad definition. With good reason. Because there are many ways of people and communities coming together; many different important issues to discuss; and many ways of reaching decisions.

WHERE DID THE WORD 'POLITICS' COME FROM?

We can thank the Greek philosopher Aristotle. He was born in 384BCE – almost 2,500 years ago – and one of his most important works, *Politiká*, addressed different approaches to **government**.

WHAT IS A GOVERNMENT?

There are many kinds of government, and different systems of democracy, which I shall discuss later, but generally when we speak of 'the government' we mean the people who are responsible for running a country, and the systems on which they rely to do so.

'JUST BECAUSE YOU DO NOT TAKE AN INTEREST IN POLITICS DOESN'T MEAN POLITICS WON'T TAKE AN INTEREST IN YOU.'

SAID BY PERICLES, AN ANCIENT GREEK POLITICIAN, BORN c.495BCE AND DIED 429BCE.

WHY SHOULD WE CARE ABOUT POLITICS?

The decisions made in politics have an impact on us, whether we like it or not. So surely it makes sense to try to have a say in those decisions, to try to have an influence on them? We can't all be Prime Minister. But we can all play a part in politics. I want to help you work out what that might mean for you.

POLITICS AFFECTS US ALL

If I listed all of the things that are decided by politicians, and especially by the government, I would need a lot more than these two pages. I'd need whole books. But here are a few of the big issues you might care about, and where politics plays a major role.

EDUCATION

- How much money is spent on schools.
- What and how you learn.
- How much you should pay for university.
- How much teachers earn.

ENVIRONMENT

- How to keep air, seas and rivers clean.
- How to meet climate targets to help the planet.

HEALTH AND WELFARE

- How many doctors and nurses there are and how much they are paid.
- Whether to invest in new hospitals and treatments.

ECONOMY

- How much money the country borrows.
- How high taxes are.

WORK

- Rights at work and help getting work.
- How to make work pay better than benefits.

DEFENCE

- How big the **army**, **navy** and **air force** are.
- Whether to go to war.

LAW AND ORDER

- How to prevent and punish crime.
- How many police we need.

HOUSING

- How to help people with nowhere to live.
- How many new houses we need and where to build them.

CULTURE

- How much to invest in theatres, libraries, museums and sport, and make them accessible.

TRANSPORT

- How much it costs to use trains and buses.
- Where roads, railways and airports are built.

INTERVIEW
METE COBAN MBE

Mete Coban, CEO of My Life My Say
(a youth-led movement encouraging young
people to get fully involved in democracy
and get every single young person voting)

WHAT GOT YOU INTERESTED IN POLITICS?

In my teens, my local youth club on our council
estate was shut down after 35 years. It was like
a second home for me and many of my friends.
It was a shock to everyone, and no one in power
lifted a finger. The whole estate felt powerless.
That moment made me realise that unless people
who look and sound like me get involved in politics,
no one will be there to voice the views of my
community. I've been a political activist ever since
and became a councillor at 21.

DO YOU WANT TO BE AN MP?

One day, yes. I founded My Life My Say when
I was 20 because I wanted to bring about change
for those who feel voiceless. I ran to be a councillor
because I wanted to support my community.
Entering politics at a national level would let me
do all that and more.

DO YOU UNDERSTAND WHY SOME YOUNG PEOPLE HAVE LOST FAITH IN THE SYSTEM?

Yes, there is a lot to be angry about. But not engaging in the system only helps those who want young people to stay away from politics. The more young people say politics doesn't matter, the less the politicians will care what they think. They listen to pensioners, that's for sure!

WHAT DO YOU SAY TO YOUNG PEOPLE WHO SAY THEIR OPINION DOESN'T MATTER?

That it can, and it will if you decide that it will, and it won't if you turn away. Because if you don't do politics, politics will do you. Housing, work, education, climate, whatever issues a young person cares about, politics is at the heart of them all, so everyone should try to have a say.

HOW CAN YOUNG PEOPLE GET THEIR VOICE HEARD?

At the very least, be registered to vote so that your presence is felt and politicians will have no choice but to create policies that appeal to young people. If we fail to engage, we risk leaving a few people to continue making decisions that serve their own interests, whilst the rest of us live with the consequences.

WHAT IS A POLITICIAN?

A politician is someone who works in politics, particularly if they are in an elected position.

WHAT SKILLS DO YOU NEED TO BE A POLITICIAN?

It takes all sorts of skills, but from my experience I would say you need: strong beliefs; a good work ethic; an ability to assess issues, people and situations; and an ability to make decisions. It helps if you can inspire and motivate, write and speak clearly, and be confident.

YOU NEED A THICK SKIN TOO. SINCE SOCIAL MEDIA BEGAN, ABUSE IN POLITICS HAS GOT WORSE AND IT CAN BE REALLY UNPLEASANT.

DO YOU NEED A DEGREE TO BE A POLITICIAN?

No. I speak in lots of schools, and it is a common misconception that you need a degree, or that you must go to private school. John Major was Prime Minister from 1990 to 1997 with just three O-levels (now called GCSEs), after leaving school at 16. Winston Churchill didn't have a degree, and he is generally considered one of the UK's greatest ever leaders. Most Prime Ministers have been to university, though.

DO YOU NEED TO GO TO A PRIVATE SCHOOL TO BECOME PRIME MINISTER?

One private school, Eton College, has produced three times more Prime Ministers than the **Labour Party** has in its entire 125-year history. However, most **Members of Parliament (MPs)** went to state schools. Don't be fooled because you have seen so many in recent years who were privately educated: Boris Johnson, David Cameron and Jacob Rees-Mogg (all Eton), Rishi Sunak (Winchester) and Jeremy Hunt (Charterhouse).

IS IT JUST CONSERVATIVES WHO WENT TO PRIVATE SCHOOLS?

No. Labour Prime Ministers Tony Blair and Clement Attlee (who beat Churchill in the first election after World War II, and whose government founded the **National Health Service (NHS)** and the **Welfare State** – *see page 66*) went to private schools. However, several Labour leaders have been from a working-class background and went to state schools.

THE GREAT THING ABOUT POLITICS IS THAT
YOU REALLY WILL FIND PEOPLE FROM
A RANGE OF BACKGROUNDS.

HAS POLITICS ALWAYS EXISTED?

If you take my definition – how people and communities make decisions that affect the issues of concern to them – then, yes. Back when our ancestors were hunter-gatherers, I imagine they argued about who should lead them, and how resources were shared. Arguments and discussions leading to decisions – that's politics. Then as people started to work out the importance of land, water and climate, tribes formed and fought over access to resources they needed to live. How wars start and how wars end – that's politics too.

HOW HAS POLITICS CHANGED?

That is a long and complicated story. But the major change has been the development of the world into a collection of nation-states, which have each created their own political systems. Though no two countries have exactly the same system, they often draw on each other's ideas and experience.

In the UK and many other countries, such as France and Germany, Australia and Canada, there are **political parties** – gatherings of like-minded people who work together (though not always!) in the pursuit of power, so that they can be in charge of making the important decisions facing the country they want to lead. (*See pages 80 and 85.*)

WHAT IS A PERFECT POLITICAL SYSTEM?

The short answer is that there isn't one. The longer answer is that it depends on your political beliefs and principles. In the UK, we are a **parliamentary democracy** (*see page 102*), yet millions of people want to change the way the system is run, for example the voting system, the voting age, and the balance of power between national and local government.

Some countries are run by **dictatorships** (*see page 104*). Whilst this may be hard to imagine, there are people who say they prefer to have an **authoritarian** leader at the top, with near total control of his country.

I DELIBERATELY SAY 'HIS' BECAUSE ALL MODERN–DAY DICTATORS ARE MEN, SUCH AS VLADIMIR PUTIN IN RUSSIA, XI JINPING IN CHINA AND KIM JONG UN IN NORTH KOREA.

THERE HAVE BEEN ALL–POWERFUL WOMEN IN THE PAST, AMONG THEM ELIZABETH I OF ENGLAND AND IRELAND, CATHERINE THE GREAT OF RUSSIA, EMPRESS WU ZETIAN OF CHINA AND CLEOPATRA OF EGYPT, BUT THEY WERE MONARCHS, NOT DICTATORS.

WHAT IS DEMOCRACY?

Abraham Lincoln, US President from 1861 to his assassination in 1865, gave what I believe is the best description of democracy, in a speech he delivered in 1863, referring to it as **'government of the people, by the people, for the people'**. The people as a whole choose who govern them by voting for them, and those who are chosen should always understand that they are there to serve the people.

> 'NO ONE PRETENDS THAT DEMOCRACY IS PERFECT OR ALL-WISE.'

WINSTON CHURCHILL, FORMER PRIME MINISTER, SAID THIS IN THE HOUSE OF COMMONS, 11 NOVEMBER 1947.

WHEN DID DEMOCRACY START?

Democracy as a way of governing began to emerge in Athens, Greece, during the fifth century. It has spread widely, but not all countries are democracies. And some countries have elections, but are not democratic e.g. Russia (*see page 106*).

THE WORD DEMOCRACY COMES FROM TWO GREEK WORDS: *DEMOS* = PEOPLE, *KRATIA* = POWER OR RULE.

WHY IS DEMOCRACY IMPORTANT?

Democracy at its best makes everyone feel that their voice counts for something. It gives freedom to speak, think and act – provided we do so within the law – and allows similar freedoms to those we don't agree with. It ensures that we are all equal in the eyes of the law. It allows us to resolve arguments and conflict peacefully. It gives us the power to elect our leaders, and then replace them if they let us down. It encourages governments and politicians to be accountable to the people.

ARE THERE ANY DOWNSIDES TO DEMOCRACY?

Just as we can elect good governments, we can elect bad governments.

THE UK HAD FIVE CONSERVATIVE PRIME MINISTERS IN SIX YEARS AFTER THE 2016 BREXIT REFERENDUM, WHICH SUGGESTS DEMOCRACY DOESN'T GUARANTEE STABILITY.

Other downsides include . . .

- It is slower to make decisions and pass laws.

- It is harder to plan for the long term because the election cycle keeps coming round.

- People can be poorly informed about the parties and their policies, and media bias and manipulation can make things worse.

HOW DOES THE MEDIA WORK IN A DEMOCRACY?

A free and fair media is vital to a healthy democracy. TV, radio and newspapers have long been important contributors to people's understanding of political issues. Social media has become increasingly significant in recent years, with both positive and negative effects: positive in that more people can get their voices heard; negative in that it has been a growing source of hate, abuse and misinformation.

WHEN DID DEMOCRACY BEGIN IN BRITAIN?

It was a long, slow process, going back centuries. The first move came with the Magna Carta in 1215, which reduced King John's power. A 'Great Council' of bishops and peers was established to advise the English king, and over time became the first Parliament of England. The first Parliament of the Kingdom of Great Britain was established in 1707 when the Kingdoms of England and Scotland were united. But few people could vote. Even after the First Reform Act of 1832, which is seen as a key moment in parliamentary democracy in Britain, only seven per cent of the adult population could vote. It would need further Acts of Parliament in 1867, 1884 and 1918 before all men could vote and another, in 1928, before women could vote, after a campaign by the **suffragettes**.

WHO WERE THE SUFFRAGETTES?

Suffrage means 'the right to vote'. The Suffragette Movement grew out of the Women's Social and Political Union (WSPU), which was founded in 1903 by Emmeline Pankhurst, her daughters Christabel, Sylvia and Adela, and a small group of women based in Manchester. They later moved to London where a national **campaign** was established and sometimes supported by men.

HOW DID THEY CAMPAIGN?

With words: debates and arguments; books and leaflets; and a weekly newspaper. But also with deeds, for example they chained themselves to government buildings and launched attacks on property. More than 1,000 suffragettes, including the Pankhursts, went to prison, and some went on hunger strike to draw attention to the campaign.

DID THEY WIN?

Yes and no. When World War I broke out in 1914, they suspended their violent actions to support the war effort. So, their campaign did not lead directly to women getting the vote. However, when that change came some years later in 1928, the Suffragettes' campaign, and the support they won for their cause, was a major reason.

WHY IS POLITICS EXCITING?

It's about things that matter. It's about people and passion. It's about teams. It's about winning and losing.

The best moment of my professional life was the moment I realised the Good Friday Agreement (*see page 47*), which helped bring peace to Northern Ireland, was happening. It felt like a miracle. Suddenly the hard work as part of the UK government team, the travel, the arguments, the late nights negotiating, all seemed worthwhile.

Then I think of election nights, the highs and the lows. Winning, and the overwhelming feeling that comes from knowing millions and millions of people have voted to make the win a reality. Followed by the joy of seeing a new school or hospital opened, a new community project funded, or new laws passed. Or losing, and knowing that if only we had been able to inspire more people to work for us, to vote for us, we would be a step closer to turning our election promises into a reality.

Also, if you get into politics, I guarantee you will make some of the most important and lasting friendships of your life.

CHAPTER 2

IN CHARGE

STRUCTURE OF THE UK GOVERNMENT

Each country has its own political system, though the UK's will be familiar to many countries, because there was a time when Britain governed almost a quarter of the world, as part of the **British Empire**. Some, like Australia, Canada and India, modelled their systems largely on ours. Others did things differently.

The UK is a constitutional monarchy, with a monarch as Head of State; but also a parliamentary democracy, in which real power rests with the elected government, headed by the Prime Minister. So the structure is . . .

THE MONARCH

The king or queen, Head of State (*see page 28*).

PRIME MINISTER (PM)

The PM is Head of Government (*see page 48*).

CABINET

The team appointed by the PM to run government departments (*see page 58*).

THE HOUSES OF PARLIAMENT ARE ALSO
KNOWN AS THE PALACE OF WESTMINSTER,
AS THEY WERE ORIGINALLY BUILT AS
A ROYAL PALACE DURING THE 11TH CENTURY.

PARLIAMENT

This consists of two Houses, where people meet to debate and vote on laws (see page 32).

HOUSE OF COMMONS

650 Members of Parliament who are elected by the people (see page 33).

HOUSE OF LORDS

786 lords and baronesses who are not elected by anyone (see page 36).

GOVERNMENT AND OPPOSITION

Government ministers sit on one side of the House of Commons. The Opposition sits opposite them (see page 51).

THE HOUSES OF PARLIAMENT WERE THE SITE OF THE GUNPOWDER PLOT (THE ASSASSINATION ATTEMPT IN 1605 OF KING JAMES I, LED BY GUY FAWKES), WHICH WE 'CELEBRATE', WEIRDLY, EVERY 5 NOVEMBER.

WHAT POWER DOES OUR MONARCH HAVE?

In the UK, the monarch has no actual political power. They cannot pass laws or choose ministers, and are not supposed to make controversial statements on political issues. However, they have 'soft power'. This a phrase given to the influence a country can have through means other than military or economic power, such as history, culture or general reputation. The huge global interest in the **Royal Family** adds to this soft power.

DID MONARCHS EVER HAVE POLITICAL POWER?

Yes, lots of it. Absolute power, in fact. That started to change with the Magna Carta. It was signed by King John in 1215 to allow barons – rich landowners – to be part of a 'Great Council' (later called Parliament) and to help make new laws.

WHAT IS ABSOLUTE MONARCHY?

A system in which the monarch has power without limits. It was common in Europe during the 17th and 18th centuries. Perhaps the most extreme was King Louis XIV of France, who reigned from 1643–1715. He was made king aged four but took on the actual role when he became an adult, and assumed absolute power in his thirties when he decided to rule without a chief minister.

> VISITORS TO KING LOUIS XIV WEREN'T ALLOWED TO KNOCK ON HIS DOOR – THEY COULD ONLY SCRATCH IT GENTLY WITH THEIR LITTLE FINGER!

WHY DIDN'T MONARCHS AFTER KING JOHN ASSUME ABSOLUTE POWER?

Well, King Charles I of England tried! He decided to rule without Parliament, which led to the Civil War from 1642–1651. He was convicted of treason, and executed for his troubles – head chopped off, if you want the detail. Charles was defeated by forces led by Oliver Cromwell (who was also convicted of treason after his death – his body was removed from his tomb and hanged!) Brutal stuff!

ARE THERE ANY MONARCHS WITH POLITICAL POWER TODAY?

Yes, several. Quite a few are in the Middle East: Saudi Arabia (perhaps the most powerful); Qatar; and the United Arab Emirates. Oh, and we shouldn't forget Vatican City, which is tiny but significant because the sovereign (person of highest power) is the Pope, head of the Catholic Church worldwide.

WHAT DOES KING CHARLES III DO?

Our current monarch, King Charles III, has ceremonial roles, which include being Head of . . . State, the Church of England, the Armed Forces and the **Commonwealth** *(see page 109)*. These institutions have an important place in our **Constitution** (the rules and traditions of the political system). Also, part of being Head of State is being a **diplomat** – representing the UK in the world and hosting world leaders when they visit.

DO WE NEED A MONARCHY?

I am not really a supporter of the monarchy, but I am in a minority in the UK. The system is broadly popular and respected, although surveys suggest young people are less supportive than older people. The Royal Family is seen by many as a symbol of stability, tradition, national identity and pride, and a major tourist attraction. It sits above politics. Polling shows it to be a huge soft power asset, and I regularly saw that at work when Queen Elizabeth II was mixing with elected political leaders from abroad.

The main arguments against it are that it is not democratic, the hereditary principle justifies class division and inequality, and it costs a lot of money to run.

CAN THE MONARCH GIVE THEIR OPINION?

Queen Elizabeth II was scrupulously apolitical (which means she didn't share her political opinions), but King Charles III established a reputation as an environmental campaigner when he was Prince of Wales, and he has carried on in the same vein. The role of the monarch has always adapted according to time and the personality of the occupant of the role. Prince William has been a very vocal campaigner on mental health and has followed his father in supporting efforts to combat climate change and protect biodiversity.

'WHEN I SETTLE ON SOMETHING [WHICH CAUSES AND EVENTS TO SUPPORT], I WANT TO DIG DEEP, I WANT TO UNDERSTAND WHAT I AM INVOLVED IN, I WANT TO UNDERSTAND THE COMPLEXITIES OF ALL THE ISSUES AND, ABOVE ALL, I WANT TO MAKE AN IMPACT.'

PRINCE WILLIAM SPEAKING IN AN INTERVIEW I DID WITH HIM FOR *GQ MAGAZINE*.

WHAT IS PARLIAMENT?

Parliament is the place in Westminster, London, where politicians debate and vote on big issues, make or change laws, and decide how public money is spent. The word parliament comes from the French verb *parler*, which means 'to talk'. There's certainly a lot of talking that goes on!

DO YOU NEED TO TALK LOUDLY TO GET YOUR VOICE HEARD?

In the olden days, yes. But these days, there are microphones to help! It can certainly get noisy in there during debates though, especially the House of Commons.

GET INVOLVED

Every word said in Parliament is transcribed and published. It is now possible to read all debates online after the event. Check out hansard.parliament.uk and find a debate on a subject that interests you.

You can watch debates live too, as Parliament has its own channel (Parliamentlive.tv).

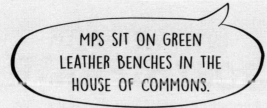

MPS SIT ON GREEN LEATHER BENCHES IN THE HOUSE OF COMMONS.

WHAT IS THE HOUSE OF COMMONS?

One of two debating chambers, it is made up of 650 Members of Parliament (MPs). They are elected, which means they are voted in during something called a **general election**, which usually takes place every four or five years (*see page 78*). It is more powerful than the House of Lords.

THE MONARCH IS NOT ALLOWED INTO THE HOUSE OF COMMONS. THIS RULE DATES TO KING CHARLES I (REMEMBER THE ONE WHO LOST HIS HEAD – SEE PAGE 29). HE TRIED TO ENTER THE COMMONS IN 1642 WITH SOME ARMED MEN TO ARREST FIVE MPs FOR TREASON (THEY HAD TRIED TO KILL THE MONARCH).

WHAT HAPPENS IN THE HOUSE OF COMMONS?

This is usually where new laws or updates to existing laws are put forward by the government, in a proposal called a **Bill**, and are then debated.

INTERVIEW WITH
RORY STEWART

Former Cabinet minister – a lifelong
Conservative – and my co-presenter on
The Rest Is Politics podcast

WHY DID YOU WANT TO BE AN MP?

I had been a soldier and a diplomat, so always
believed in public service, and I have always been
interested in politics. Being an MP, you are literally
at the service of the public who elect you.

WHAT MADE YOU A CONSERVATIVE?

I believe in evolutionary change, and see a huge
role for tradition, such as monarchy, protection
of landscape, respect for institutions.

IF YOU COULD CHANGE ONE THING, WHAT WOULD IT BE?

There should be greater freedom for MPs to
genuinely speak their minds, and vote with
their consciences, rather than be pressured
to follow a party line.

WHAT DID YOU LIKE ABOUT BEING A MINISTER?

Responsibility. Making decisions. Being able
to immerse myself in issues.

WHAT DID YOU NOT LIKE ABOUT BEING A MINISTER?

Literally being thrown into important positions without proper handover or training, and suddenly expected to be an expert on things you knew very little about.

YOU LEFT PARLIAMENT BECAUSE BORIS JOHNSON EXPELLED YOU FOR THE STANCE YOU TOOK AGAINST HIS POSITION ON BREXIT. DO YOU REGRET THAT?

I would like to have had a longer career in Parliament, and as a minister. But I could not serve under Johnson, who I believe to be an amoral person, and I have no regrets about that.

DO YOU MISS POLITICS?

Yes and no. Though I am no longer an MP, I still feel engaged in politics. By writing, speaking and doing the podcast, I make sure I keep abreast of issues.

WOULD YOU RECOMMEND GOING INTO POLITICS TO A YOUNG PERSON?

I would, but with their eyes open, and with an understanding that so much needs to change, and we need a new generation willing to take a new approach and change it.

WHAT IS THE HOUSE OF LORDS?

It is the second of two debating chambers in Parliament, made up of almost 800 unelected lords and baronesses (also known as peers). Some inherited their titles, but most are appointed by political parties, and especially by the PM.

THESE UNELECTED PEERS SIT ON RED LEATHER BENCHES IN THE HOUSE OF LORDS.

THERE IS A LOT OF DEBATE ABOUT WHETHER THE SYSTEM SHOULD CHANGE BECAUSE IT SEEMS SO OLD-FASHIONED AND UNDEMOCRATIC THAT PEERS ARE NOT ELECTED. SUPPORTERS ARGUE THIS IS TO ENSURE THE HOUSE OF COMMONS REMAINS THE MORE IMPORTANT CHAMBER. WHAT DO YOU THINK?

THE AVERAGE AGE OF MEMBERS OF THE HOUSE OF LORDS IS 69. THE YOUNGEST MEMBER IS 28 – A MEMBER OF THE PLAID CYMRU PARTY CALLED CARMEN SMITH WHO WANTS TO ABOLISH THE HOUSE OF LORDS!

WHAT DOES THE HOUSE OF LORDS DO?

It can ask the government and the House of Commons to think again about decisions they have made or to make changes to proposed legislation.

WHAT IS PMQs?

This stands for **Prime Minister's Questions**, which takes place in the House of Commons at midday every Wednesday when Parliament is sitting.
It is one of the few occasions in the parliamentary week when the Commons is packed.

WHAT IS THE POINT OF PMQs?

It is a chance for MPs to ask the Prime Minister anything, from serious issues of foreign and economic policy, to local issues and events in their constituencies. It is also when the big themes of political debate get honed and sharpened. A fair chunk of the session is taken up by the **Leader of the Opposition**, who is allowed six questions.

DOES THE PM KNOW QUESTIONS IN ADVANCE?

MPs from their own side might let the PM's team know, and very occasionally so will an Opposition MP, but generally, NO. However, it is usually fairly easy to work out what the Leader of the Opposition is likely to ask about.

PMQs USED TO BE TWICE A WEEK, FOR 15 MINUTES. NOW IT IS WEEKLY, FOR HALF AN HOUR. IN SOME COUNTRIES, IRELAND AND AUSTRALIA FOR EXAMPLE, THE PM HAS TO GO TO PMQs EVERY DAY.

WHY CAN PMQs BE FRUSTRATING?

The main complaints are: 'I wouldn't let my kids behave like that' and 'Why doesn't the Prime Minister actually answer the questions?' Certainly, it gets very rowdy. The **Speaker**, who is like the referee in a sporting event, tries to keep order, but both sides like to put the other side off their stride, and shouting and yelling and trying to drown out the PM or the Leader of the Opposition are common tactics. It's actually pretty pointless because, provided the person speaking gets close to the microphone, their voice will carry. As for not answering questions, it is usually either because they don't want to admit the facts, or they want to turn their answer into an attack on the person who asked the question. That's pointless too, because it is so obvious they're not answering the question.

MPs HAVE TO CALL EACH OTHER 'HONOURABLE' AND THEY CAN'T CALL ANOTHER MP BY THEIR NAME OR SAY 'YOU', BECAUSE MPs HAVE TO SPEAK 'THROUGH THE CHAIR', I.E. ADDRESS THEMSELVES TO THE SPEAKER.

(THEY'RE NOT ALLOWED TO CALL ANOTHER MP A LIAR EITHER!)

TIPS FOR ASKING A QUESTION

Be sure about your facts. Don't waffle. Frame the question so it demands a direct answer.

MPs BOB UP AND DOWN TO TRY TO CATCH THE SPEAKER'S EYE, SO THAT THEY MIGHT BE CALLED TO ASK A QUESTION.

TIPS FOR ANSWERING A QUESTION

Be sure about your facts. And that means putting in the work needed to have all the answers at your fingertips. The PM usually has a giant folder with a mass of information and suggested answers.

WHAT'S INSIDE THE HOUSE OF COMMONS?

THE SPEAKER'S CHAIR

The Speaker presides over the House of Commons. When the Speaker stands, MPs are supposed to sit. Their chair, which stands four metres tall, was a gift from Australia, to replace a Speaker's chair destroyed in World War II.

CLERKS' TABLE

This is in front of the Speaker's chair. It is where the Clerk of the House, who is the senior official, and two assistants, sit and advise the Speaker and indeed MPs, on proceedings.

GOVERNMENT FRONT BENCH

Government ministers occupy the front bench to the right of the Speaker, up to the aisle halfway down the chamber.

OPPOSITION FRONT BENCH

The Opposition MPs (*see page 51*), who 'shadow' government ministers by acting as their party's spokespeople on specific issues, occupy the front bench to the left of the Speaker.

DESPATCH BOX

These are lecterns from which government and Opposition frontbenchers speak.

THE MACE

A symbol of Royal authority, carried into the House at the head of the Speaker's procession every day that Parliament is in session. A number of MPs through time have removed the mace as a form of protest, among them Oliver Cromwell, former Tory deputy PM Michael Heseltine, and more recently Labour MP John McDonnell.

BACKBENCHERS

Backbench MPs are neither ministers nor shadow ministers. They sit wherever they can on the remaining benches.

PRESS AND PUBLIC GALLERIES

Both press (journalists) and the public can watch proceedings from galleries above the chamber. I sat in the press gallery when I was a journalist. What a view I had!

INTERVIEW
SIR LINDSAY HOYLE

Speaker of the House of Commons

HOW DOES SOMEONE BECOME THE SPEAKER?

You must be an MP and elected to the post by other MPs, usually at the start of a new Parliament after a general election. The Speaker is usually an experienced MP who has served in the House for many years and can work with MPs of all parties. Once you become the Speaker, you are expected to resign from your former political party and be neutral from then onwards. I was elected as Speaker in 2019.

WHAT DOES THE SPEAKER ACTUALLY DO?

My most visible role is to chair proceedings in the chamber and enable backbenchers to hold the government of the day to account. This involves choosing who speaks in debates or asks questions at Question Time. The Speaker decides which amendments to government Bills are debated, and whether to grant urgent questions on matters of high importance. The Speaker also maintains order in the chamber.

WHAT DOES THAT INVOLVE?

Ensuring all procedure rules are followed properly. While debates can get extremely passionate, and sometimes the noise is off the scale, I always try to emphasise that the watching public are not impressed by bad behaviour, especially if the voice of the person speaking is drowned out.

ARE YOU ALLOWED TO PUNISH MPs WHO MISBEHAVE?

Occasionally, if an MP refuses to accept the authority of the Speaker, or breaks rules and refuses to apologise, I can order them to leave the House. I've had to do that a few times.

WHAT IS THE BEST THING ABOUT YOUR JOB?

I love Parliament, and representing the people of Chorley, Lancashire, but it is also an unbelievable privilege to be Speaker and centrally involved in the democratic process.

WHAT IS THE WORST THING ABOUT YOUR JOB?

It is not always possible to call everyone who wants to speak or ask a question, so I am always having to disappoint people. Also, I worry about the safety and security of MPs. So many suffer abuse and harassment in their constituencies and through social media. I am working hard with different authorities to ensure we can defend our democracy.

WHO DECIDES WHICH BILLS ARE PUT FORWARD?

Mainly the government. Each year, it puts together a list of the new laws it wants to bring in. This is presented to MPs and peers by the king, sitting on a throne in the House of Lords. It is known as The King's Speech, because it is read by the king.

THE KING HAS TO BE APOLITICAL, SO HAS NO SAY IN THE SPEECH'S CONTENT. IT IS WRITTEN BY POLITICAL OFFICIALS AND ADVISERS, AND SIGNED OFF BY THE PM AND OTHER MINISTERS.

The speech sets out the Bills (proposed new laws), which will be debated several times in both Houses, and by committees of MPs. When the process is done, the king signs them into law, and the Bills become **Acts of Parliament** (the laws of the land). Around 25 to 50 new **Acts** are passed each year.

MY FAVOURITE IS THE NATIONAL MINIMUM WAGE ACT 1998 — A LAW THAT MAKES IT ILLEGAL TO PAY PEOPLE VERY LOW WAGES. THIS TOOK ALMOST 100 YEARS OF TRYING BY THE LABOUR PARTY!

Ordinary MPs can also put forward laws through Private Members' Bills. MPs must enter a ballot to have their Bill chosen, and very few make it into law. They are more a way of raising issues.

DID YOU KNOW?

Sometimes laws remain even if they are no longer relevant, simply to avoid Parliament having to undo what has been done. For example, it is unlikely anyone will commit to changing a 1313 Act that declares MPs cannot wear a suit of armour inside Parliament!

WHAT DO MPs DO IF THEY'RE NOT IN DEBATES?

Constituency work, networking, reading, making visits . . . Also, a lot of the real work in Parliament goes on in committees, groups of MPs looking at a particular issue or Bill, often by questioning ministers, civil servants (*see page 60*) and experts. These tend to be more calm!

WHAT IS CONSTITUENCY WORK?

MPs are answerable to the local people who elected them, and they hold regular surgeries so that constituents can debate with them or bring them problems they need help with. Common issues are housing, benefits (*see page 68*), planning and anti-social behaviour. MPs also employ people to help with these, called case workers.

ARE SCOTLAND, WALES AND NORTHERN IRELAND GOVERNED IN THE SAME WAY AS ENGLAND?

No. They are all part of the UK, they send MPs to the UK Parliament in Westminster, and are covered by many laws made there. But they also have their own governments and their own parliaments (called the Assembly in Northern Ireland), also elected. These have responsibility for many of the government services, like schools and hospitals, transport and police. The leaders of these governments are called **First Ministers**, so they don't get confused with the Prime Minister.

IN 1707, SOMETHING CALLED THE ACTS OF UNION BROUGHT TOGETHER THE SEPARATE KINGDOMS OF ENGLAND AND SCOTLAND. AT THE TIME, WALES WAS PART OF ENGLAND. NORTHERN IRELAND WAS ADDED IN 1921 (THE REPUBLIC OF IRELAND WON INDEPENDENCE FROM BRITAIN IN 1920).

WHY DON'T THESE COUNTRIES GO IT ALONE?

Many would like to as they believe they would be better off and better governed if they were responsible for all laws in their own countries.

Plaid Cymru, a Welsh political party, argues for independence.

The **Scottish National Party (SNP)**, which has dominated Scottish politics since first winning power in 2007, is fighting for a **referendum** – a general vote on a single issue (*see page 103*). However, only the UK government can agree to a referendum. In 2014, a referendum on Scottish independence was won 55 per cent to 45 per cent by those wishing to remain part of the UK.

Northern Ireland has long been the subject of intense debate and sometimes violence. More than 3,500 people died between the late 1960s and late 1990s, in violence between Nationalists, mainly **Catholics** who wanted to be part of the Republic of Ireland, and **Unionists**, mainly **Protestants**, who wished to remain part of the UK. The violence was largely ended by the **Good Friday Agreement** in 1998, which allowed people to identify as British or Irish, but kept Northern Ireland as part of the UK. The debate about Northern Ireland's status continues to this day, but much more peacefully.

WHAT DOES THE UK PRIME MINISTER DO?

A lot! The Prime Minister is the **Head of Government** – responsible for all government policy and decisions. They also decide who runs other government departments, and ultimately they have the final say in the big decisions facing the government. It is a position with enormous power, which is why it is important that people of real quality and principles make it to Downing Street.

In recent years, that has not always been the case.

BORIS JOHNSON BECAME THE FIRST PM IN HISTORY TO BE BANNED FROM PARLIAMENT BECAUSE HE LIED ABOUT COVID PARTIES IN PARLIAMENT. JOHNSON WAS FOLLOWED AS PM BY LIZ TRUSS, WHO LASTED JUST 49 DAYS IN OFFICE.

SINCE 1735, THE OFFICIAL HOME AND OFFICE OF THE PRIME MINISTER HAS BEEN 10 DOWNING STREET, IN LONDON. THE PM ALSO HAS ACCESS TO A COUNTRY ESTATE, CHEQUERS, SET IN BEAUTIFUL BUCKINGHAMSHIRE COUNTRYSIDE.

IS A GENERAL ELECTION NEEDED FOR SOMEONE TO BECOME UK PRIME MINISTER?

No. When Tony Blair stepped down as PM in 2007 after ten years, Gordon Brown took over and he replaced him as Leader of the Labour Party, which already had a majority in Parliament, so, as part of the democratic process, Queen Elizabeth II asked him to form a government.

And of the five recent Conservative Prime Ministers, only one, David Cameron, first became Prime Minister directly as a result of a general election. Theresa May, Boris Johnson, Liz Truss and Rishi Sunak all became PM by winning a party leadership election, following the resignation of their predecessor. May and Johnson later fought a general election.

A PM HAS GREATER AUTHORITY IF THEY HAVE LED THEIR PARTY TO A WIN.

THERE IS A LOT OF FOCUS ON PARTY LEADERS DURING AN ELECTION CAMPAIGN, SO A LEADER WHO BECOMES PM BY WINNING A GENERAL ELECTION HAS CONSIDERABLE POLITICAL STRENGTH AS A RESULT. THE WIN IS VERY MUCH SEEN AS THEIRS. THAT GIVES THEM ADDITIONAL AUTHORITY WITH BOTH THE PUBLIC AND MPs.

WHO DECIDES WHO THE LEADERS OF THE PARTIES ARE?

It varies, but for the main parties, it is basically a mix of MPs and party members who vote for the leader. In both the Conservative and Labour parties, the leader must be an MP. In the Labour Party, votes are shared between different groupings made up of MPs, trade unions and party members. In the Conservative Party, MPs decide which of the would-be leaders are the top two, and these are then voted on by the party members.

DID YOU KNOW?

There have been calls to change the way party leaders are chosen because in several recent leadership elections, the choices of party activists have not been as popular with the general public who, ultimately, get to decide which party leader becomes PM. Jeremy Corbyn was popular with many Labour activists, but rejected by the public. Liz Truss was popular with many Tory activists, but a disaster as PM.

WHAT DO YOU THINK?

HOW DOES A PARTY WIN AN ELECTION?

It is basically a numbers game. The UK is divided into 650 areas called parliamentary constituencies (sometimes referred to as seats). Different parties put forward candidates, the public in each area votes for their favourite, and the one who gets the most votes is elected to Parliament as the MP for that constituency. In some constituencies, called **safe seats**, MPs have enormous **majorities**. In others, called **marginal seats**, the results are much closer. These tend to be the seats that decide the outcome of the election.

The leader of the party with the most MPs gets the first go at trying to form a government. If their party has more winning candidates than the other parties combined, they have a majority, and the leader of that party becomes Prime Minister.

WHAT DO THE MPs OF LOSING PARTIES DO?

They represent their constituencies, and together form the Opposition in Parliament. The leader of the losing party with the most seats becomes the Leader of the Opposition, whose role is to hold the government to account, which means challenging and questioning, as well as putting forward alternative ideas for debate. Being leader of the Opposition is good training for being PM!

INTERVIEW WITH
KEIR STARMER
Leader of the Labour Party

DID YOU ALWAYS WANT TO BE A POLITICIAN?
No. I had an ordinary working-class childhood.
My dad was a toolmaker and my mum was a nurse,
but she became very ill when I was still at school,
and looking after her became my dad's main focus.
They were interested in politics, but it wasn't the
biggest thing in our lives.

WERE YOU ALWAYS LABOUR?
Yes. I studied law at university and took a special
interest in human-rights law. I've always had
a strong belief in justice, knowing the difference
between right and wrong, and feeling that we
are here to help others, not just ourselves. To me
those are strong Labour values.

WHEN DID YOU WANT TO BE A POLITICAL LEADER?
I never thought of it in those terms. I became
Director of Public Prosecutions, which is an
important legal role in the government, running
the Crown Prosecution Service. Over time, the idea
of becoming an MP became more interesting to me.

DO YOU ENJOY YOUR JOB?

It's a privilege but it is hard work. And I cannot say Opposition has ever been truly enjoyable. You have to be in government to make real change.

WHAT DO YOU DO AWAY FROM THE JOB?

My family are unbelievably important to me. Politics is so all-consuming, but I try to make sure we have time together as a family. My other passion is football.

HAS SOCIAL MEDIA MADE POLITICS HARDER?

I think it has. Women in particular get appalling abuse. You have to have a thick skin, but it is also important not to lose empathy because most people are totally decent and good people.

WOULD YOU ENCOURAGE YOUR CHILDREN TO GO INTO POLITICS?

I would encourage them to do whatever they think will satisfy them most. But to any young person who was thinking about politics, I would definitely encourage them to go for it. It is hard, but there are few things more rewarding in life than standing up for other people and making a difference for the better in their lives. That is what has always motivated me and always will.

QUIZ: WHAT KIND OF LEADER ARE YOU?

Imagine you're in charge of a litter pick.
Pick option a, b or c for each question to see
what kind of leader you might be.

1. One member of your team is working more slowly than the rest of the group. Do you ...

a) Get your best litter picker to work alongside them, to advise and encourage?

b) Spend some time watching them to gather more information?

c) Ask them if they are struggling with anything and what might help?

2. The first area is now clean – everyone has done a great job. Do you ...

a) Move on to the next area?

b) Think about strategies for how to improve when your group moves to the next area?

c) Tell everyone to take a break and suggest some games to play together (they've earned a rest)?

3. Some people have complained that their litter picking tools aren't working. Do you ...

a) Go to your teacher and ask for different tools?

b) Take a look at the tools to find out if there is a way to fix them?

c) Gather your group together to find out if everyone is having the same problem – maybe it's just a couple that are broken?

4. Two people are having an argument and have stopped litter picking. Do you ...

a) Tell them to litter pick in separate areas so they can cool off?

b) Ask how the argument started – perhaps you can help them to resolve it?

c) Tell them to sort out their problem, with help from the teacher if needed – the rest of the group can keep going and get the job done?

Turn over to see whether you're a decisive, thoughtful or collaborative leader . . .

If you answered . . .

MOSTLY As = DECISIVE LEADER

You make decisions and like to get things done quickly and efficiently. Being decisive can be a good thing, but make sure it doesn't get in the way of building good relationships.

MOSTLY Bs = THOUGHTFUL LEADER

You like to spend time thinking and finding out information before making any decisions. This can pay off – it's better to make the right decision over a bit more time rather than a rash split-second choice. Just make sure you don't get so caught up in thinking that you don't make a decision at all!

MOSTLY Cs = COLLABORATIVE LEADER

You put the team first and want to make sure everyone can give their best to a project. Being a good listener is important, as is working together effectively. Just remember that being a leader can also be about making tough decisions that not everyone will like.

THE BEST LEADERS HAVE A BIT OF ALL OF THE ABOVE. THEY CAN MAKE DIFFICULT DECISIONS. THEY THINK HARD. AND THEY UNDERSTAND AND VALUE THE IMPORTANCE OF THE TEAM.

CHAPTER 3

HOW GOVERNMENT WORKS

WHAT HAPPENS AFTER THE PM IS VOTED IN?

Often the first thing the Prime Minister does after arriving in 10 Downing Street is to appoint the **Cabinet** – the top ministers who run the main government departments. This is made up mainly of Members of Parliament (MPs) and sometimes Members of the House of Lords.

IN THE CABINET ROOM AT 10 DOWNING STREET, THERE IS A HUGE OVAL TABLE. THIS DESIGN ALLOWS THE PRIME MINISTER TO SEE THE FACES OF ALL THE MINISTERS WHO ARE PRESENT AT MEETINGS.

WHAT DO CABINET MINISTERS DO?

Also known as **Secretaries of State**, the Cabinet ministers are responsible for running the main government departments. They progress new laws relating to their departments, appear regularly in Parliament to be asked questions about their work, and sit on committees with other ministers about issues that concern more than one department. They have teams of junior ministers, who are responsible for different areas of work within each department. And they have civil servants working for them (*see page 60*).

GOVERNMENT DEPARTMENTS

The **24 UK GOVERNMENT DEPARTMENTS** include health, education, transport, environment, culture, business, work and pensions, housing and local government, and justice. The main ones are:

THE TREASURY: The most powerful department, led by the **Chancellor of the Exchequer**. It is where the big decisions about money are made. Other ministers are always arguing for money from the Treasury for their departments.

THE HOME OFFICE: Responsible for law and order, and the safety of the country.

THE FOREIGN OFFICE: Deals with the UK's relations with other countries and addresses international issues.

THE MINISTRY OF DEFENCE: In charge of the military.

GET INVOLVED

What new department would you create and why? E.g. Department for children, Department for Artificial Intelligence (AI), Department for Sorting Out Brexit (SOB!).

WHAT DO CIVIL SERVANTS DO?

Civil servants work for the civil service, which supports government ministers in developing and implementing their ideas and policies. They are politically impartial, which means they work for whichever government the country elects. Though elected ministers set out policy and direction, often civil servants run the services on which we all depend, such as benefits and pensions, or organising driving licences or passports.

'CIVIL SERVANTS MUST LEAVE THEIR OWN POLITICS AT THE DOOR WHEN THEY ARRIVE FOR WORK. THEY ARE THERE TO SERVE THE COUNTRY, AND THE GOVERNMENT THE COUNTRY ELECTS. THEY ARE ENTITLED TO – AND THEY MUST – CHALLENGE MINISTERS WHEN THEY HAVE DOUBTS OR WORRIES ABOUT A POLICY OR DECISION. BUT THEY ARE ADVISERS. ADVISERS ADVISE. MINISTERS DECIDE.'

FROM LORD GUS O'DONNELL, FORMER HEAD OF THE CIVIL SERVICE.

HOW DO CIVIL SERVANTS HELP MAKE LAWS?

Let's imagine a government was elected on a promise to ban vaping.

I'D VOTE FOR THAT!

The minister would require civil servants to prepare a Bill to be put before Parliament.

THIS WOULD INVOLVE SPEAKING TO EXPERTS TO WORK OUT THE BEST WAY OF IMPLEMENTING THE BAN. THEY WOULD ALSO HELP TO PREPARE ANSWERS TO ANY DIFFICULT QUESTIONS AND THINK OF RESPONSES TO POSSIBLE ATTACKS UPON IT BY OPPONENTS, SUCH AS 'IT'S ANTI–FREEDOM', 'VAPING HELPS PEOPLE STOP SMOKING' AND 'VAPING HELPS THE ECONOMY'.

Once the Bill is going through Parliament, and the government is persuading MPs and peers to back it, civil servants will be tracking the progress, and helping the minister deal with the different positions taken by others, and sometimes adapting the policy as it gets debated in the Commons, the Lords, in committees, and across the media.

HOW MUCH MONEY DOES THE GOVERNMENT SPEND?

A lot. As things stand, the government raises and spends more than one trillion pounds each year. A trillion is one thousand billion, which is: £1,000,000,000,000. The total spending planned for 2024 was close to £1.2 trillion. That works out at around £16,000 per person.

WHERE DOES IT ALL COME FROM?

Mostly from taxation, and also borrowing.

HOW DO GOVERNMENTS BORROW MONEY?

Governments borrow from the financial markets – mainly pension funds and insurance companies. These financial institutions lend money to the government in the form of bonds. Bonds represent a promise to repay the money that has been borrowed with interest on top.

IN THE UK, THESE BONDS ARE CALLED 'GILTS' AND ARE SEEN AS VERY SAFE INVESTMENTS BECAUSE THE GOVERNMENT HAS ALWAYS PAID BACK INTEREST AND PAYMENTS ON GILTS TO THE INSTITUTIONS FROM WHICH IT HAS BORROWED.

WHERE DOES ALL THE TAX MONEY COME FROM?

The biggest chunk – a quarter – comes from **Income Tax**, which is money paid to the government on earnings over a certain threshold.

The next big earner is **Value Added Tax (VAT)**, which is paid on goods and services that we buy.

And the third big tax-raiser is **National Insurance**, which is also a tax on earnings, and used for certain benefits – such as the State Pension.

These three taxes account for almost half of the money raised in tax. Taxes on **business profits**, **alcohol**, **tobacco** and **energy**, **council tax** and **repaid student loans** help to make up the rest.

DO WE PAY ENOUGH TAX?

One of the biggest political questions! If we want good schools and other public services, we need money from taxes to fund them. Equally, many argue that high taxation can damage business and families' spending and so harm economic growth. Governments have to try to get the balance right.

MANY PEOPLE, INCLUDING SOME OF THE RICHEST, AVOID PAYING TAX BY USING CLEVER LAWYERS AND ACCOUNTANTS. WHY DON'T THEY PAY THEIR FAIR SHARE?

WHERE DOES THE MONEY ALL GO?

Imagine £1,200 billion (this is the 1.2 trillion I mentioned on p60) in the form of a cake . . .

The **NHS AND THE WELFARE STATE** make up around 50 per cent of the cake (around £600 billion).

The next biggest slice is **EDUCATION** at 11 per cent (£131 billion).

Then comes the cost of **BORROWING.** In 2024, paying the interest on the money the government has borrowed will cost ten per cent (£116 billion).

DEFENCE takes around six per cent (£68 billion). This is likely to increase in the coming years, especially because of the threat posed by Russia.

TRANSPORT is five per cent (£62 billion). Roads, railways, ferries – things that keep the UK moving.

ONE PHRASE YOU WILL HEAR A LOT IS GDP. IT STANDS FOR GROSS DOMESTIC PRODUCT AND BASICALLY MEANS HOW MUCH MONEY A COUNTRY IS WORTH.

PUBLIC SPENDING IS OFTEN CALCULATED IN TERMS OF 'SHARE OF GDP'. IN THE UK, PUBLIC SPENDING MAKES UP JUST OVER 40 PER CENT OF GDP. FRANCE IS A LOT HIGHER — WELL OVER 50 PER CENT — THE USA IS LOWER — IN THE MID–30s.

INDUSTRY, EMPLOYMENT AND AGRICULTURE account for four per cent (£50 billion).

LAW AND ORDER e.g. police, the courts, dealing with terrorism, that's four per cent (£47 billion).

HOUSING AND THE ENVIRONMENT
Where we live, the air we breathe, big stuff like that, takes three per cent (£38 billion).

GET INVOLVED

Imagine you are Prime Minister, and you want to spend £10 billion more on defence, without putting up taxes. What area would you spend less on? Go online and do some research. What if you decided to give £10 billion to a different department — what might they spend the extra money on?

WHAT IS A WELFARE STATE?

The Labour post-war government created the modern welfare state (*see page 17*). Welfare systems are about making sure that the poorest people still have access to the basics they need for living – like food, shelter and medical treatment when they're ill. There had been welfare systems before that, but the big change was the acceptance that the **State** – i.e. government – has a responsibility to provide basic economic and social security for all people.

HOW DOES IT PROVIDE THIS SECURITY?

Through systems of benefit (financial) support. In 1942, during World War II, William Beveridge wrote a ground-breaking report identifying five 'Giant Evils' – squalor, ignorance, want, idleness and disease. He suggested a compulsory insurance scheme so that benefits could be paid to the unemployed, pensioners, widows and children in poverty. His ideas became the basis for Labour's approach to welfare. Although the Giant Evils still exist, progress made by the creation of the welfare state, alongside free healthcare for all at the point of use via the National Health Service (NHS), means that the post-war government is seen as one of the most significant in the UK's history.

WHAT IS HAPPENING WITH THE NHS NOW?

It is under massive pressure. Doctors and nurses have been on strike for better pay and conditions. The NHS waiting lists for treatment have gone as high as seven million people. Many people struggle to see a family doctor or a dentist.

IS THE NHS BROKEN?

It remains an incredible service. The NHS sees about 1.3 million people every day, so expectations can't always be met. The NHS is not broken, but needs more support. Both in terms of money and the need to reform and modernise. This is where technology, including Artificial Intelligence (AI), could be a game-changer.

WHAT DO YOU THINK? IF YOU WERE IN CHARGE, WHAT WOULD YOU DO WITH THE NHS?

WHAT IS PRIVATISATION?

Privatisation is where private companies, rather than the State (government), are in charge of public services. This is different to public-private partnerships, where the State uses private companies to help deliver the care people need.

WHAT BENEFITS CAN PEOPLE CLAIM TODAY?

Among the main benefits are . . .

UNIVERSAL CREDIT supports people on a low income.

JOBSEEKER'S ALLOWANCE for people who have little or no work.

STATE PENSION for everyone 66 or over who has contributed National Insurance payments (*see page 63*).

PENSION CREDIT to top up the State Pension.

PERSONAL INDEPENDENCE PAYMENT (PIP) for people with physical or mental health conditions or disabilities that make it difficult for them to get around and do everyday things.

Who can receive what will depend on factors such as age, income, work status and health.

THE WEEKLY STATE PENSION
IS CURRENTLY £221.20, WHICH WORKS
OUT AT £11,502.40 A YEAR.

WHAT IS SOCIAL HOUSING?

Social housing is rented housing for people on low incomes or with particular needs. It is provided by landlords who are registered with the Regulator of Social Housing, usually a local council or a housing association. The social housing provided by councils is sometimes referred to as **council housing**.

WHAT IS AFFORDABLE HOUSING?

Affordable housing is cheaper housing for those who couldn't otherwise afford somewhere to live. There is affordable rented housing, where rents are lower than most private rented properties, and affordable housing people can buy. Affordable housing for sale is sold at between 20 per cent and 50 per cent less than the market price for that type of property, or sometimes through schemes that make it easier for those on lower incomes to buy.

IS THERE A HOUSING CRISIS?

Yes, in that we have record levels of homelessness, and young people in particular are finding it harder and harder to buy a home or to rent at levels they can afford. The population has grown, but we have not built enough new homes.

HOW DOES THE GOVERNMENT HELP SCHOOLS?

Education for 93 per cent of pupils is funded by the government. The money pays for everything required to run a school. The government also decides how much teachers are paid, what they teach, and the exams pupils do. The other seven per cent use private schools, paid for independently, not by the government. Private schools have greater freedom in how they are run.

DO SCHOOLS GET ENOUGH MONEY?

I am sure headteachers would always welcome more. In state schools, the average spend per child per year is around £8,000. Whereas in private schools, it is almost double – about £15,200.

CAN CHILDREN INFLUENCE HOW THEIR SCHOOL IS RUN?

Lots of schools have a school council, whose members are elected from the student population. It can be a great way to learn about campaigning, but also you can have ideas and argue for them to be taken up. Check out if your school has one. If not, why not start one?

WHAT ABOUT ARTS AND CULTURE?

There is a specific government ministry called the **Department for Culture, Media and Sport**. Support comes mainly through government funding of the Arts Council (the national development agency for creativity and culture). Arts and sport also benefit from funding via the National Lottery, set up by the government to raise money for 'good causes'.

DO THE ARTS GET ENOUGH SUPPORT?

Many people feel that with more support, culture could generate even more money for the UK – already a world leader in music, film, theatre, literature etc.

'THE ARTS ARE A BIG PART OF WHAT
MAKES LIFE SPECIAL. BRITAIN IS
RENOWNED FOR CULTURE AND
CREATIVITY. BUT I SOMETIMES FEEL
POLITICS VIEWS CULTURE AS A LUXURY,
RATHER THAN THE NECESSITY,
FOR EDUCATION AND FOR
THE ECONOMY, THAT IT IS.'

FROM KEIRA KNIGHTLEY,
ACTOR.

71

HOW IS CRIME DEALT WITH?

The government funds the police, border and security services (e.g. MI5 – the domestic security service). They have the job of preventing crime, pursuing criminals who commit crime, and keeping the country safe. Government sets the general approach, but the police have operational independence, which means they cannot be directly told what to do or how to do it.

'THE THREATS FROM HOSTILE STATES, TERRORISTS AND ORGANISED CRIMINALS CHANGE AND EVOLVE. THE SECURITY AND INTELLIGENCE AGENCIES AND THE POLICE TRY TO KEEP AHEAD OF THEM AND ADAPT. PUBLIC SUPPORT FOR THIS WORK AND PUBLIC VIGILANCE WILL ALWAYS BE AN IMPORTANT PART OF OUR DEFENCE AGAINST THESE THREATS.'

FROM DAME ELIZA MANNINGHAM-BULLER, FORMER HEAD OF MI5.

HOW DO LAW COURTS OPERATE?

Law courts are funded by the government, but judges are independent. If police charge someone with a crime, it is up to a court of law, presided over by a magistrate or judge, sometimes with a jury of 12 ordinary people, to decide whether the defendant is innocent or guilty. The government sets guidelines on what sentences judges and magistrates should impose, though they do have the right to apply their own judgement, within limits. The government is also responsible for prisons, though some are run by private companies.

WHO IS IN CHARGE OF THE ARMED FORCES?

Constitutionally, the king, as he is **Head of the Armed Forces**. However, it is the Prime Minister and the **Secretary of State for Defence** who are in charge politically, and the **Chief of Defence Staff** who is in charge of the military. The UK has an army, a navy and an air force, and is also one of a small number of countries with nuclear weapons. The UK is a member of NATO (the North Atlantic Treaty Organisation), and a lot of the defence work is done in co-operation with other countries.

NATO IS AN ALLIANCE OF 32 COUNTRIES FORMED AFTER WORLD WAR II. A MILITARY ATTACK ON ONE IS SEEN AS AN ATTACK ON ALL.

HOW SHOULD THE GOVERNMENT PROTECT THE ENVIRONMENT?

The government is responsible for trying to protect the environment: assuring water and air quality; regulating waste produced by businesses and households; treating land contaminated by substances (e.g. chemicals); ensuring we have adequate fish stocks; and helping conserve the natural world. Two government departments share the challenges facing the environment: the **Department for Environment, Food and Rural Affairs**; and the recently established **Department for Energy and Net Zero**.

NET ZERO IS THE BALANCE BETWEEN THE GREENHOUSE GASES WE PUT INTO THE ATMOSPHERE, MAINLY BY THE BURNING OF FOSSIL FUELS LIKE OIL, GAS AND COAL, AND THE AMOUNT THAT WE REMOVE FROM THE ATMOSPHERE, FOR EXAMPLE BY PRESERVING OR PLANTING FORESTS.

WHY HAS NET ZERO BECOME A POLITICAL ISSUE?

I don't know! It seems odd to me that there are politicians, campaigners and businesses that refuse to accept the science that overwhelmingly states the climate crisis as a threat, which requires us all to make change.

ARE GOVERNMENTS DOING ENOUGH TO HELP FIGHT CLIMATE CHANGE?

There is a big drive to move from fossil fuels to renewables and create energy from solar and wind. And more than 40 countries have introduced carbon taxes, making businesses that cause greenhouse-gas emissions, such as coal-fired power plants, to pay for the damage they cause and encouraging them to produce less pollution. The argument against it is that it piles more tax on business and stops the economy growing. But Sweden was one of the first countries to bring in a national carbon tax in 1991, since when emissions there have been cut by 27 per cent, and the economy has grown well. Could other countries do the same?

WHY IS WATER QUALITY A POLITICAL ISSUE?

A rise in sewage spills into our rivers has led to calls for privatised water companies to be brought back into public ownership. Water and sewage were sold off by the Conservative Prime Minister Margaret Thatcher in 1989, one of several utilities her government privatised. She said it would lead to a new era of investment, improve water quality and help bring down bills. Even her biggest supporters would be hard pressed to say this has worked out. Water and rail have the strongest public support for a return to greater government control.

HOW DOES THE GOVERNMENT DEAL WITH A CRISIS?

When a crisis occurs, the whole weight of government must be used to deal with it. The UK manages crises from **COBRA**, which sounds like something from a scary movie, but in fact stands for **Cabinet Office Briefing Room A**. It is a place where ministers and advisers can have access to data and information in real time. This allows them to make the decisions needed to manage the crisis.

THE COVID-19 PANDEMIC WAS AN
EXAMPLE OF A CRISIS THAT HIT
EVERY COUNTRY, AND THEREFORE EVERY
GOVERNMENT IN THE WORLD.

HOW OFTEN DOES A CRISIS HAPPEN?

The media talk of things being in crisis all the time, but during the ten years I worked with former Prime Minister Tony Blair, we had dozens of very difficult situations, but I think only six that I would describe as a real crisis. For example, the Iraq War, the 9/11 terrorist attacks in New York in 2001, and when we had to destroy six million cows due to disease in the same year.

CHAPTER 4

ELECTIONS AND VOTING

ARE ALL ELECTIONS THE SAME?

No. Just like governments, they vary from country to country. There are many similarities – for example, people vote! But there are more differences: in voting system; rules covering who can or can't vote; and the length of campaigns.

HOW OFTEN ARE UK GENERAL ELECTIONS HELD?

Every few years. The maximum a government can stay in power without holding a general election is five years – long enough for a government to get settled in, make change and hopefully plan for the long term. Australia and New Zealand have three-year terms. I've yet to meet a politician there who doesn't want to change it. They say three years – the rule in their Constitutions – means they are always thinking about the next election!

WHO DECIDES WHEN ELECTIONS ARE HELD?

The Prime Minister (usually when they think they have the best chance of winning!). When they name the date, they go to the monarch to ask for Parliament to be **dissolved** (the official term for the end of a Parliament before a general election), and then the campaign begins (the official campaign that is, the unofficial campaign begins earlier!).

HOW LONG DO ELECTION CAMPAIGNS LAST?

Between three and six weeks. That doesn't sound long, but they are exhausting, especially for party leaders, who travel around the country, do events, meetings, speeches, debates, interviews and visits. UK elections take place in a day, always on a Thursday.

WHY ARE UK ELECTIONS HELD ON A THURSDAY?

Tradition – dating back to a different world. In many places, Thursday was market day so people would be out and about. Today, many countries hold elections at the weekend, when people might have more spare time.

DID YOU KNOW?

US presidential campaigns are longer. They take place every four years, in November, but candidates often begin campaigns over a year in advance. During this gruelling process, called the primaries, politicians seek to become their party's candidate and campaign all over the country. The presidential election itself takes place over a single day.

WHAT ARE THE UK'S MAIN POLITICAL PARTIES?

The Conservatives and Labour. The **Liberal Democrats** have often been called 'the third party', but in recent years the Scottish National Party (SNP) has had more seats in Parliament than the Liberal Democrats, even though the SNP stands only in Scotland. Wales also has a nationalist party, Plaid Cymru. And the Green Party has grown in recent years.

Northern Ireland has its own parties, largely reflected in the historic argument between **Unionism** – people who want to stay part of the UK – and **Nationalism** – people who want to be part of the Republic of Ireland (*see page 47*). Currently, the two main parties in Northern Ireland are Sinn Féin (Nationalist), and the Democratic Unionist Party (Unionist). Their leaders work together trying to run the government of Northern Ireland under a system known as power-sharing.

THERE ARE FUN PARTIES TOO.
COUNT BINFACE OF THE COUNT BINFACE PARTY
(HE WEARS A DUSTBIN OVER HIS HEAD) WON MORE
THAN 24,000 VOTES WHEN HE STOOD TO BE LONDON
MAYOR IN 2024. AMONG HIS POLICIES WAS BANNING
NOISY SNACKING IN THEATRES. NOW THAT IS
A POLICY I SUPPORT!

WHAT IS LEFT WING AND RIGHT WING?

These terms date to the French Revolution in 1789. In the French National Assembly, supporters of the old system under an all-powerful king sat on the right; supporters of the Revolution on the left. Today, it relates more to people's basic political outlook:

A LEFT-WING PERSON IS MORE LIKELY TO BELIEVE IN THE ROLE OF GOVERNMENT IN ADDRESSING SOCIAL AND ECONOMIC INEQUALITY. THE LABOUR PARTY LEANS LEFT.

A RIGHT-WING PERSON BELIEVES MORE IN THE FREEDOM OF THE INDIVIDUAL AND THE ECONOMIC MARKET. THE CONSERVATIVE PARTY LEANS RIGHT.

A centrist person is likely to sit somewhere between the two, and will tend to support one of the smaller parties, or one of the two main parties if their policies are leaning more to the centre.

QUIZ: ARE YOU MORE LEFT WING OR RIGHT WING?

For each scenario, pick the statement
that is closest to your own view.

1.

a) Everyone who works should pay reasonable
   levels of income tax (*see page 63*), to fund
   public services like schools and hospitals.

b) Taxes should be low because people who
   work hard should be able to keep most
   of the money they earn.

2.

a) Private education is bad because it gives
   those who can afford to pay fees an unfair
   advantage over children from poorer families.

b) Opposition to private schools is nothing more
   than class war.

3.

a) Big businesses make too much profit.

b) Corporations deserve the fair profits
   they make.

4.

a) The National Health Service (NHS) is one of the country's greatest achievements and we should not undermine its basic principle – healthcare for all, at the point of need, regardless of ability to pay.

b) We cannot go on spending so much of taxpayers' money on the NHS and should introduce a new system to pay for it, including charges for some services.

5.

a) It is shameful that we dropped the commitment to spend 0.7 per cent of GDP on overseas development.

b) Why should we spend more on foreign countries when we have so many problems in the UK?

6.

a) Crimes happen because society has failed people, so prison is a place where they should be rehabilitated to become better citizens.

b) People make their own choices – if they choose to commit crimes, they should pay the consequences with harsh sentences.

Turn over to see if you're more left wing or right wing in your outlook.

If you answered . . .

MOSTLY As = YOU LEAN MORE TO THE LEFT WING

To quote the Labour Party Constitution, you want 'power, wealth and opportunity' to be 'in the hands of the many, not the few'. So you lean to Labour, but you might also be attracted by the Liberal Democrats or the Green Party. The Liberal Democrats are passionate about changing the voting system; the Greens are passionate about protecting the environment.

MOSTLY Bs = YOU LEAN MORE TO THE RIGHT WING

You put more faith in the individual than the collective. That would chime with the Conservative Party, though they are also being challenged in some parts of the country by the recently created Reform Party, which is further to the right.

The parties have policies on most issues, and for many people, they like some things about one party, other things about another. But when it comes to a general election, you can only vote for one!

ALL THE PARTIES HAVE WEBSITES, WHERE YOU CAN CHECK OUT THEIR POLICIES AND PROMISES. IT IS ALWAYS GOOD TO CHECK THEIR CLAIMS ON A RANGE OF FACT-CHECKING SITES.

HOW CAN I TELL THE DIFFERENCE BETWEEN POLITICAL PARTIES?

They have different policies, which are set out in documents called **manifestos**. A manifesto explains all the plans a party intends to implement if they are elected. The parties publish them early in the campaign, then try to promote the ideas positively, while their opponents try to pick them apart during the election campaign.

A bit like sports teams, the political parties have their own colours, for example:

CONSERVATIVES = BLUE
LABOUR = RED
LIBERAL DEMOCRATS = YELLOW/ORANGE
SCOTTISH NATIONAL PARTY = YELLOW
PLAID CYMRU = YELLOW AND GREEN
GREEN PARTY = GREEN (NO SURPRISE THERE!)
SINN FÉIN = GREEN
DEMOCRATIC UNIONIST PARTY = RED, WHITE AND BLUE

THAT'S WHY WE WENT FOR PINK ON THE COVER!

Parties also have logos, and they sometimes change these to move with the times or to grab attention. Labour's red flag was changed in 1987 to a red rose to soften the image. The Conservatives under David Cameron changed from a flaming torch to an oak tree to signal greater commitment to the environment.

DO WE VOTE FOR A PARTY OR AN INDIVIDUAL?

People vote for all sorts of different reasons. For many, it is about the party. For others, what matters is the quality of the candidates, and who they think will be best for their local area. Who the party leaders are is important because they could be Prime Minister one day. Also, during a campaign so much of the focus is on the leaders, not least when they debate each other on TV.

HOW DO I DECIDE WHO TO VOTE FOR?

Take it seriously. Read widely. Talk to other people about the issues. Check out the parties' plans and the candidates in your constituency. In the run-up to an election, candidates have teams of volunteers who knock on doors to persuade people to vote for them and deliver leaflets setting out their plans. Read what they are promising.

In most constituencies, there will be **hustings** (events where the candidates debate in front of live audiences). Try to get to one, see the candidates in action and compare their policies and characters.

IF YOU KNOW LONG BEFORE AN ELECTION WHO YOU ARE BACKING, THINK ABOUT BECOMING A VOLUNTEER, HELPING YOUR CHOSEN CANDIDATE TO WIN.

HOW ARE THE CANDIDATES CHOSEN?

In every constituency, local parties will select their candidates, though the parties nationally might also have a say. They are usually selected well before the election is called. **Independent candidates** (*see page 94*) rarely win, but many choose to stand, often to campaign on a single issue. The last MP to be elected on a single local issue was Dr Richard Taylor, in 2001 and 2005, who won in Wyre Forest, on saving Kidderminster Hospital's Accident and Emergency Department.

WHEN A CANDIDATE BECOMES AN MP, DO THEY HAVE TO FOLLOW THE POLICIES OF THE LEADER?

There is an expectation that MPs will vote for plans set out in the manifesto, and a team of MPs – called **whips** – try to ensure their colleagues back the government, with a mix of threats and persuasion. But sometimes MPs rebel and vote against the government on an issue they feel strongly about. Ministers cannot do this. They are bound by **collective responsibility**, which means they can argue against a policy in private, but once it is government policy, they must support it, or resign. For example, when Theresa May was PM, Foreign Secretary Boris Johnson and Brexit Secretary David Davis resigned because of their opposition to her proposed Brexit deal.

HOW OLD DO YOU NEED TO BE TO VOTE?

It depends. For a UK general election, it's 18.
For Scottish and Welsh parliamentary and local
elections, it's 16. The world's highest voting age
is 25, in the United Arab Emirates.

WHO CAN VOTE?

In the UK, you must be either a British citizen,
a qualifying Commonwealth citizen or a citizen
of the Republic of Ireland. You must be registered
to vote, and you must have photo ID.

IS VOTING COMPULSORY?

It is in some countries, such as Australia. In most
countries, including the UK, it is voluntary. There
are some countries, such as Brazil, where it is
compulsory for everyone between 18 and 70,
but voluntary for those aged 16–18 or over 70.

GET INVOLVED

If you are 16 or older (14 in Scotland
and Wales), go online and register on the
government website. It won't take long!
If you are younger, look at the process.

ARGUMENTS FOR COMPULSORY VOTING:

Supporters feel that it gives greater strength to those who are elected, and that it has an educational benefit (people take more interest in politics if they have to vote). Whenever I visit Australia, politicians and people also tell me that they feel compulsory voting makes it harder for populists and extremists to win support.

ARGUMENTS AGAINST COMPULSORY VOTING:

Democracy is about freedom, and that should include the freedom of the individual not to take part. Also, some people are not interested in politics and don't want to make a decision on something they don't know much about.

WHAT HAPPENS ON ELECTION DAY?

All over the UK, **polling stations** open at 7am and close at 10pm. They are set up in schools, village halls and other public buildings.

SOME PEOPLE WILL ALREADY HAVE VOTED BECAUSE IT IS POSSIBLE TO VOTE BY POST IN ADVANCE OF ELECTION DAY.

WHAT HAPPENS AT THE POLLING STATIONS?

Voters are sent a **poll card** in advance telling them where to vote. At the polling station, they give their name and address to officials, and show their photo ID.

PHOTO ID IS A NEW AND CONTROVERSIAL DEVELOPMENT THAT CRITICS BELIEVE WAS DESIGNED TO DETER YOUNGER AND POORER PEOPLE FROM BEING ABLE TO VOTE. WHAT DO YOU THINK?

Voters will then be given a **ballot paper** with a list of all the candidates in their constituency. They go into a private booth, put a cross in the box next to the name of the candidate they want to vote for, and then put their ballot paper into a **ballot box**.

POLL WORKERS CHECK EACH VOTER AND HAND THEM THE BALLOT PAPER – THERE IS ALSO A BRAILLE VERSION FOR PEOPLE WITH SIGHT LOSS.

CAN YOU SEE HOW OTHER PEOPLE VOTE?

It is a secret ballot, but voters are free to tell anyone they like who they voted for, or they can keep it secret if they prefer.

WHAT DO POLITICIANS DO ON ELECTION DAY?

Politicians are not allowed to campaign publicly on election day itself and there are restrictions on media reporting too. So, for the candidates and their teams, the day is spent either waiting impatiently, or making sure people who have promised to vote for them get to the polling stations and vote (called GOTV – Get Out The Vote).

HOW DOES 'GET OUT THE VOTE' WORK?

It might involve phone calls, visits to the homes of potential voters, and the offer to help get them to the polling station. In the close constituency contests that might decide the overall election, this can be the difference between winning and losing. It's why party activists are so important.

WHEN DO WE GET THE ELECTION RESULTS?

It's possible to get a good idea of the results as soon as the polls close at 10pm, because polling companies spend the day asking people how they voted (called **exit polls**). Counting the votes starts immediately, and the actual results start to come in around midnight, constituency by constituency. Although it can be the weekend before all the votes are counted (UK elections always happen on a Thursday – *see page 79*), a picture forms quickly of what is happening, and who is likely to win.

IN 1997, IT WAS OBVIOUS EARLY ON THAT LABOUR HAD WON A HUGE MAJORITY WELL BEFORE ALL VOTES WERE COUNTED. THE LOSING PRIME MINISTER, JOHN MAJOR, TELEPHONED TONY BLAIR TO CONCEDE DEFEAT. I WAS WITH TONY AT THE TIME. HE WAS WEARING A RUGBY SHIRT, SHORTS AND SLIPPERS, SO IT DIDN'T FEEL LIKE A MOMENT IN HISTORY!

DO VOTES EVER NEED TO BE RECOUNTED?

Yes, sometimes when a result is very close in a particular constituency, a candidate can ask for a recount. There have been cases, mostly in local elections, where the result has been a tie, and has been decided by the toss of a coin!

HOW QUICKLY DOES A CHANGE OF GOVERNMENT TAKE PLACE?

In the UK, it can be the next day! You go from a long, exhausting campaign, a night without sleep as the results come in, then you're into government doing some of the most difficult jobs! In the US, there is a transition of a couple of months. In many countries, especially those with a system of **proportional representation (PR)**, it can take weeks or months. Under PR, the votes of the party as a whole dictate how many seats they get (*see page 94*), so they negotiate deals on policy and personnel before agreeing to form a government.

BELGIUM WENT FROM DECEMBER 2018 TO OCTOBER 2020 — 652 DAYS! — WITHOUT A GOVERNMENT AS THE PARTIES NEGOTIATED. THE CIVIL SERVICE HAD TO RUN THINGS WITHOUT THEM.

WHAT'S A BY-ELECTION?

A **by-election** takes place when a constituency loses its MP between general elections. This might be because of death, resignation, bankruptcy, conviction of a serious criminal offence, or the MP taking a seat in the House of Lords. Also, a new system was recently introduced, known as **recall**, which allows constituents to force their MP to leave, if they are found guilty of wrongdoing.

WHAT IS THE VOTING SYSTEM IN THE UK?

It is called **First Past the Post (FPTP)**. This is how it works . . . The parties select a candidate to stand in each of the 650 constituencies. (Some have independent candidates who are not part of a political party and some have candidates from parties that exist only in one or a few areas.) Voters then vote for the candidate they want to represent them in Parliament. Whoever gets the most votes in a constituency wins and becomes the MP for that seat.

ARGUMENTS FOR FIRST PAST THE POST:

- Simple and familiar. One person = one vote.
- Individual MPs represent every area of the UK.
- A party can form a stable government without needing a majority of votes nationwide.
- Helps keep extremists out of Parliament.

ARGUMENTS AGAINST FIRST PAST THE POST:

- Unfair, because results are not proportionate to votes. If 20 per cent vote for a party, shouldn't that party should get 20 per cent of the seats?
- Favours big parties, who can secure a majority of seats without winning a majority of votes.
- It is much harder for smaller parties to get representation in Parliament.

WHY NOT CHANGE THE SYSTEM?

Plenty of people would like to, but it has often benefited the two main parties to keep it as it is.

IN LABOUR'S THIRD ELECTION WIN, IN 2005, THEY HAD A MAJORITY OF MPs IN PARLIAMENT, EVEN THOUGH THEY ONLY WON 35 PER CENT OF ALL THE VOTES CAST. IN 2015, THE CONSERVATIVES WON A MAJORITY WITH JUST 37 PER CENT.

That 2015 election is a good example of why people say the FPTP system is unfair . . .

PARTY	VOTE SHARE	NUMBER OF SEATS
Liberal Democrats	7.9%	eight seats
UK Independence Party	12.6%	one seat
SNP	4.7%	56 seats
Conservatives	36.9%	330 seats
Labour	30.4%	232 seats

GET INVOLVED

Would you vote to change the voting system or keep First Past the Post? Speak to family and teachers, and do some research to help with your decision. And see pages 96–97 for information about alternative voting systems.

IF THE ELECTION SYSTEM CHANGED, WHAT WOULD IT CHANGE TO?

What critics of First Past the Post want is something called **proportional representation (PR)**. There are various possible PR systems, but the basic idea is that the seats in Parliament are in closer proportion to the votes cast.

More countries use proportional representation than First Past the Post – more than 100 compared with fewer than 50 – the latter mainly countries that used to be under British rule.

HAS THE UK EVER TRIED TO CHANGE THE ELECTION SYSTEM?

The Liberal Democrats have long campaigned to change the voting system, and as part of the **Cameron–Clegg coalition** (*see page 99*) there was a referendum asking the country if it wanted to replace First Past the Post with an **Alternative Vote (AV) system**: 67.9 per cent voted to keep things as they are (though many didn't vote, including people who now complain about First Past the Post. If only they had voted at the time!).

WHAT IS ALTERNATIVE VOTING?

Alternative Voting (AV) is a form of proportional representation (PR), in which you rank candidates in order of preference. The winner must get more than 50 per cent. But if nobody does, the one with the fewest first choice votes is eliminated, and their second choice votes are added to the tally of the candidates still in the race. And so on until someone has more than half of the votes.

WHAT SYSTEMS DO THE SCOTTISH AND WELSH PARLIAMENTS USE?

Scotland and Wales have systems that combine First Past the Post and proportional representation (PR). Every voter has two votes: one for their constituency to choose an individual candidate, who wins on First Past the Post; and one for their region, where the number of seats across a region relates to the percentage of votes cast (PR).

WHAT SYSTEM DOES THE NORTHERN IRELAND ASSEMBLY USE?

Northern Ireland uses a PR system called **Single Transferable Vote (STV)**.

WHAT HAPPENS IF NO PARTY GETS A MAJORITY IN A GENERAL ELECTION?

If no party gets a majority (at least one more than half the seats – *see also page 51*), there can be a **coalition government**, or a **minority government**.

A COALITION GOVERNMENT IS ONE IN WHICH TWO OR MORE PARTIES COMBINE TO FORM A GOVERNMENT THAT CAN COMMAND A MAJORITY IN PARLIAMENT.

A minority government is one in which the party with the most seats tries to govern the country without having a majority in Parliament (fewer than 50 per cent of the seats).

DID YOU KNOW?

Theresa May ran a minority government after failing to win a majority in 2017. She then had to rely on the support of the Democratic Unionist Party from Northern Ireland to stay on in government. This gave the DUP's ten MPs disproportionate power.

HOW OFTEN DOES A COALITION HAPPEN?

There have been just six in total, mainly in wartime.

UK COALITION GOVERNMENTS

The first coalition since World War II was formed after five dramatic days following the inconclusive 2010 general election. The Conservatives won the most seats – 306 – but not enough for a majority. Labour won 258 and the Liberal Democrats 57, which even combined was short of a majority. But with Labour quite close to the Liberal Democrats on many issues, Prime Minister Gordon Brown sought to persuade the Lib Dems that they should try to govern together. Their leader Nick Clegg was at the centre of a tug of war as both Gordon Brown and Conservative leader David Cameron tried to win him over. Secret meetings were held to thrash out possible agreements on policy and Cabinet positions. I was with Gordon Brown in Downing Street when he finally accepted it was all over. Clegg later told me the election result numbers just didn't add up.

Gordon Brown went to see Queen Elizabeth II at Buckingham Palace to resign. After 13 years, Labour was out of power. The queen then asked Cameron to form a government. His first decision was to appoint Nick Clegg as Deputy Prime Minister. They governed together for five years before Cameron's Conservatives won a majority in 2015. The coalition was done.

HOW DOES LOCAL GOVERNMENT WORK?

We vote for councillors in local elections. There are various sorts of councils, from parish council to borough council, and some cities and regions also have elected mayors.

'I LOVE THE OPPORTUNITY TO MAKE LIFE BETTER FOR LONDONERS, BUT IT CAN BE FRUSTRATING BECAUSE I HAVE LIMITED POWERS. IN TOKYO, THE MAYOR IS REPONSIBLE FOR 70 PER CENT OF ALL SPENDING ON SERVICES. IN LONDON, IT IS SEVEN PER CENT!'

SADIQ KHAN, MAYOR OF LONDON (2016 TO PRESENT).

WHAT DO COUNCILS DO?

National government raises money, and decides how it is spent, for example, how much goes on education. But it is likely to be local government that is responsible for running your school. Local authorities also raise money through council tax, business rates and charges for things like car parking. The money is used for different services: necessities like keeping streets clean and emptying bins; looking after people who need social support; and things that make life special, like parks.

CHAPTER 5

WORLD POLITICS

ARE ALL COUNTRIES GOVERNED THE SAME WAY?

No. Far from it. There are various systems of government, from full-blown democracy to **totalitarian dictatorship** (*see page 104*), and everything in between.

WHAT FORMS OF DEMOCRACY ARE THERE?

The UK is a parliamentary democracy, in that our votes elect the MPs, not the Prime Minister directly (as well as being a constitutional monarchy, *see pages 26 and 28*).

The US and France are examples of **presidential democracy**, in which the public elect the president to be head of state and head of government, like a kind of king and prime minister combined.

Germany is a **constitutional democracy**, with a written constitution that sets out the roles and responsibilities of all the different branches of government, and judges have the power to decide if those responsibilities are being met by the elected politicians.

These all have elements of **representative democracy**, where people vote for others to take decisions on their behalf, and the politicians' performance can be judged in elections.

WHAT IS DIRECT DEMOCRACY?
Direct democracy is a form of government in which laws are decided by a majority of all those eligible to vote, rather than by a body of elected representatives. There were forms of direct democracy in ancient Greece and ancient Rome.

ARE THERE ANY DIRECT DEMOCRACIES TODAY?
Switzerland gets close. Some call it a direct democracy, others a semi-direct democracy. They have elections, but citizens also have the right to vote on specific issues, and so vote on average around four times a year, often in a referendum.

WHAT IS A REFERENDUM?
A referendum is a form of direct democracy, in which the public vote on a YES–NO question to decide a policy. So for the Brexit referendum, Parliament legislated to pass the decision on whether to remain in the European Union to a vote of the people as a whole.

WHAT IS A DICTATORSHIP?

A dictatorship is a form of government in which one person or a small group of people have total control. **Totalitarianism** and **authoritarianism** are extreme forms of dictatorship, with a leader who must be obeyed, and citizens have few rights and no real say in how the country is run.

North Korea is led by dictator Kim Jong Un, whose father and grandfather ran the country before him; **no opposition is allowed**; there is no free media; and no freedom to leave the country. The UK sees the country as a threat, but does have some trade relations and an ambassador based there. (see page 107)

China is one of the world's most populous countries and yet there is only one Party allowed – **The Communist Party of China** – which controls most aspects of people's lives. Their leader, Xi Jinping, has enormous power and is set to be president for life. China is a powerful country, which is one of the reasons why, despite differences, countries like the UK do a lot of trade with it.

WHAT IS COMMUNISM?

Communism was inspired by German philosopher Karl Marx and formed the basis of the governing of the Soviet Union, which followed the old Russian Empire. It had several dictatorial leaders, notably Joseph Stalin, who was general secretary of the Communist Party from 1922 to his death in 1953. The governments of China, North Korea, Cuba, Laos and Vietnam are Communist.

DID YOU KNOW?

Karl Marx is buried in London's Highgate Cemetery. He lived and died in London after being expelled from Germany in 1849 because his views were seen as dangerous.

WHY DO SOME COUNTRIES CONTROL THE MEDIA?

Some authoritarian leaders – like Vladimir Putin in Russia or Xi Jinping in China – keep a firm control on the media, which includes shutting down newspapers and broadcast stations and putting journalists in jail. This is because they know that the media can influence people's attitudes to them and the decisions they take, and their grip on power.

ARE THERE OTHER FORMS OF DICTATORSHIP?

Yes. **Theocracy** is rule by religion. An example is Iran, where the constitution and justice systems are based on Islamic law and the president is supreme leader.

THERE ARE CURRENTLY SIX COUNTRIES RULED BY THEOCRACY: AFGHANISTAN, IRAN, MAURITANIA, SAUDI ARABIA, VATICAN CITY AND YEMEN.

CAN A DICTATORSHIP ALSO BE A DEMOCRACY?

Not really. There is something called **autocratic democracy**, in which democratic institutions seem to exist, but they are essentially just for show. Russia today under President Vladimir Putin is a good example. Putin has elections but the outcome is known before the votes are cast. He has near total control of the media and the courts.

Opponents who pose a real threat are silenced, prevented from standing for election, often jailed or killed. The body count includes opposition leader Alexei Navalny, ex-spy Alexander Litvinenko (poisoned by Putin's agents in London) and Boris Nemtsov. I was especially saddened when Nemtsov, who I got to know when he was deputy PM and who offered hope of a reformed Russia, was murdered near Putin's government base in 2015.

WHICH ARE THE WORLD'S MOST DEMOCRATIC AND LEAST DEMOCRATIC COUNTRIES?

The **Economist Intelligence Unit (EIU)** has a Democracy Index that tracks this very question. Whilst I was writing this book, Norway was named as the most democratic. In fact, five of the top ten were from Scandinavia – Iceland, Sweden, Finland and Denmark were third, fourth, fifth and sixth. New Zealand was second. Ireland was eighth. The UK was 18th.

The least democratic countries were named as Afghanistan, Myanmar, which is a **dictatorship under military control**, and North Korea.

To some extent this is a matter of opinion, but democracy is not just about free and fair elections with a real choice. It is about human rights and basic freedoms, and respect for the rule of law.

Try to imagine what it must be like to live in a country where women are denied basic freedoms (Afghanistan, for example), where protesters are brutalised (Russia and China), where only one belief system is permitted (Iran), or where no criticism of the regime is allowed and children are brainwashed to love the supreme leader (North Korea). We can have lots of complaints about politics in the UK, but compared with all of the above, we are lucky.

HOW DO COUNTRIES WORK TOGETHER?

Every country in the world has its own government. They must work with each other to solve problems that do not respect borders, such as climate change, cross-border crime or international terrorism (violence or threats of violence to try to influence the governments or to intimidate the public).

All countries must be conscious of the many security risks facing the world, and so governments work with other like-minded governments. All this falls under what is called **diplomacy** or **international relations**.

And all countries are also trying to generate wealth so that their people can have a good standard of living, which means working with other countries on business and trade.

MAJOR COUNTRIES LIKE THE UK HAVE EMBASSIES AND AMBASSADORS IN MOST OTHER COUNTRIES OF THE WORLD. OTHER COUNTRIES HAVE EMBASSIES, CONSULATES (LIKE MINI EMBASSIES) AND AMBASSADORS IN THE UK.

WHAT ARE EMBASSIES FOR?

An embassy is a little piece of your own country in a foreign land. If you are a British citizen abroad and need urgent or emergency help, for example if you lose your passport, get arrested, or have a serious accident, the British embassy in the country you're in ought to be able to help.

They also have people (diplomats and ambassadors) whose job is to liaise with the government of the country in which they are based, on issues like trade, business, agriculture, crime or defence. UK ambassadors usually have an official residence. My favourites are in Paris, Washington and Dublin.

WHAT IS AN AMBASSADOR?

Ambassadors (called **high commissioners** in Commonwealth countries) are senior diplomats. They head up the embassies, represent Britain abroad, and ensure the government in London is aware of what is happening in the country where they are based.

THE COMMONWEALTH IS AN ASSOCIATION OF 56 COUNTRIES THAT PURSUE COMMON INTERESTS. MOST OF THESE COUNTRIES ARE FORMER TERRITORIES OF THE BRITISH EMPIRE.

WHAT IS A DIPLOMAT?

A diplomat is someone who represents their own country's interests at home and abroad, whatever their own views are. They also support visiting royal, political, business and cultural figures.

WHAT MAKES A GOOD AMBASSADOR?

A good mind, the ability to get on with people, the ability to immerse yourself in another country's politics and culture, the ability to make sure the government is made aware of anything that might impact on our own political, economic or military priorities.

HOW COULD I BECOME AN AMBASSADOR OR A DIPLOMAT?

Ambassadors are usually senior diplomats who have risen through the **Foreign Office** – the full title is Foreign, Commonwealth and Development Office (FCDO). The Foreign Office is based in London, on the other side of Downing Street to Number 10, but sends people all over the world.

DO DIPLOMATS NEED TO KNOW THE LOCAL LANGUAGE WHERE THEY WORK?

It is highly recommended, but not compulsory. The Foreign Office runs a language immersion service, and many diplomats speak several languages.

WHAT HAPPENS WHEN WORLD LEADERS MEET BUT DON'T SPEAK EACH OTHER'S LANGUAGES?

They use **interpreters**. Sometimes they will be translating through an earpiece or headset used by the leaders. Other times they will sit between the leaders. But some leaders insist on having their own interpreter, so there will be two interpreters in a meeting between two people. Interpreters have to be able to keep a secret because they are often privy to discussion of deeply sensitive issues, like military plans, big economic developments, or what they think of other leaders.

Being an interpreter is a challenging role because words in negotiations are so important, and often complex and technical issues are being discussed.

I REMEMBER A DINNER ATTENDED BY PRESIDENTS CLINTON, YELTSIN AND CHIRAC (USA, RUSSIA, FRANCE), WHERE ONE OF THE INTERPRETERS THREW UP HIS HANDS AND SAID: 'I CAN'T COPE. THEY ARE ALL TALKING TOO FAST, AND AT THE SAME TIME!'

HOW DO PROBLEMS BETWEEN COUNTRIES GET RESOLVED?

Many disputes are resolved through direct dialogue and negotiation, by pressure from other countries – usually the bigger ones – or through the **United Nations** (*see page 114*) or other regional or international institutions.

WHAT IF COUNTRIES CAN'T AGREE?

Often, sadly, countries don't agree, and that is what sometimes leads to war.

WARS TEND TO HAPPEN WHEN CONFLICTS CANNOT BE RESOLVED BY DIPLOMACY.

We live in a relatively peaceful country, but we know conflict is never far away, and as the Israel–Gaza and Russia–Ukraine wars have shown, events abroad inspire strong passions at home.

WHAT POLITICAL ISSUES CAN LEAD TO WAR?

There have been many wars through history, and different reasons for them, such as: a desire for power; a dispute over land and who it belongs to; a desire for economic gain; revenge; arguments over religion; nationalism; and self-defence.

SOMETIMES A BREAKDOWN OF INTERNAL
POLITICS CAN LEAD TO CIVIL WAR, WHICH
IS WAR WITHIN A COUNTRY RATHER THAN
BETWEEN COUNTRIES.

HOW MANY WARS ARE HAPPENING RIGHT NOW?

More than 100, large and small scale. According to
the United Nations, in 2024 the world was facing
the highest number of violent conflicts since World
War II, with two billion people — a quarter of
humanity — living in places affected by conflict.

CAN WAR EVER BE JUSTIFIED?

It should always be a last resort and never entered
into lightly, but I believe it can be justified. Few
would argue that Britain was wrong to wage
war against Germany when Hitler was seeking to
conquer Europe. And though the West did not want
war with Russia over Ukraine, the US and its allies
are supporting Ukraine – partly out of fear that if
Putin wins, he will wage war elsewhere too.

WHAT IS THE UNITED NATIONS?

The United Nations (UN), whose headquarters is in New York, was established in October 1945, with the goal of preventing another world war. Today, 193 countries are members, and it lists its main purposes as: maintaining international peace and security; protecting human rights; delivering humanitarian aid; supporting sustainable development and climate action; and upholding international law.

WHY CAN'T THE UNITED NATIONS RESOLVE ALL CONFLICTS?

Because the United Nations is not a government, or a court, and it cannot pass binding laws. It is a gathering of all countries, and each one has its own differing views, interests and alliances.

WHEN THE UN WAS ESTABLISHED, FIVE COUNTRIES – THE US, THE UK, FRANCE, RUSSIA AND CHINA – WERE GIVEN SPECIAL STATUS AS PERMANENT MEMBERS OF THE SECURITY COUNCIL (THE MAIN DECISION-MAKING BODY). THEY ALL HAD, AND CONTINUE TO HAVE, THE RIGHT TO BLOCK – OR VETO – ANY DECISION THEY OBJECT TO.

If there is a vote and all countries agree except for one of the five member states, it won't succeed.

WHY THOSE FIVE?

Because they had been deemed to be the winners of World War II. They also had the first — and the most — nuclear weapons. In recent years, the UN has become more divided, with the US and the UK being politically very close to each other on most issues, France being quite close to them, and China and Russia generally hostile to the views of all three. This has led to calls for reform, but any one of the five could veto any plan to do so!

WHICH IS THE MOST POWERFUL COUNTRY IN THE WORLD?

If you ask most Americans, they will say the US. Ask a Chinese person though, and they might say China. One of the many causes of tension in the world is the struggle between the US and China for dominance. In the end, these are matters of judgement, but it is between those two. China's power has increased massively in recent years, but the US is probably more powerful in the eyes of most analysts. Who knows for how much longer though!

WHICH ARE THE POWERS OF THE FUTURE?

India, Nigeria, Brazil and Indonesia are among countries likely to be major global powers.

WHAT WAS THE BREXIT DEBATE ABOUT?

It was about whether the UK should remain a member of the European Union, which we joined on 1 January 1973, when it was better known as the 'Common Market'. The debate had raged for years inside the Conservative Party, but became a cause of heated argument for the whole country when David Cameron put the question to a referendum (*see page 103*) in 2016.

WHAT DOES THE EU DO?

Now made up of 27 countries, it defines its purpose as promoting peace, shared values and the wellbeing of its people; and giving people freedom to live and work anywhere inside the EU, whilst protecting external borders.

WHAT'S WRONG WITH THAT?

I would argue, nothing. But opponents felt that it meant the UK was giving up too much control over our own laws. They argued that membership represented lost sovereignty – that is the power to make our own laws in our own Parliament – because being in the EU involved joint decisions with other countries across many issues.

HOW DID THE REFERENDUM COME ABOUT?

Former Prime Minister David Cameron believed an 'IN–OUT?' referendum was the only way to resolve the issue 'once and for all'. He promised this in the 2015 election, which he won, so he was duty-bound to hold the referendum. The opinion polls suggested the **Remain campaign** would beat the **Leave campaign**. That turned out to be wrong. Leave won by 51.89 per cent to 48.11 per cent.

WHY DID LEAVE WIN?

Big question! The campaign was pretty awful on both sides. Leave told lots of lies. Remain tried to scare people. 'Project Lies' beat 'Project Fear'.

WHAT HAPPENED AFTER THE VOTE TO LEAVE?

Cameron resigned, saying that having argued so strongly against Brexit, he was not the right person to implement it. Theresa May replaced him but failed to persuade Parliament or her party to back the Brexit deal she negotiated, and she resigned too. Boris Johnson had led the Leave campaign, and the Conservatives elected him leader, so he became Prime Minister and led the party as the country left the EU.

HOW IS IT GOING POST BREXIT?

It is not easy to find people who say it is going well. It is now more difficult to trade with Europe. The UK government's economic experts, the Office for Budget Responsibility, reckon Brexit has reduced the UK economy by four per cent, which means we are poorer.

It has also made Britain less powerful in the world because a lot of influence came through its role as a leading member of the EU.

And although those who argued for Brexit insist we now have greater freedom to do things we want to do, and total control of our laws, Brexit has made it more difficult to live, work and travel in Europe.

I HOPE BRITAIN WILL REJOIN THE EU ONE DAY, BUT IT WILL BE A BIG CHALLENGE TO MAKE THAT HAPPEN.

DID YOU KNOW?

No other country has tried to leave the EU since Brexit. And several countries are trying to join.

CHAPTER 6

HOW YOU CAN GET INVOLVED

WHAT IF I'M TOO YOUNG TO VOTE?

Even if you are not old enough to vote, you are old enough to have opinions and get involved. Taking an interest is being involved. Reading widely. Being curious about the world around you, past, present and future. Follow the news and make sure you listen to and read different reports and views.

CAN I BELIEVE WHAT I READ OR WATCH?

Be alert to the possibility that content might not be what it seems. Use sources you trust. Check things if you are going to repeat them, rely on them or base decisions on them. Check where you saw a piece of information – do you trust the site/channel/publication? Who put it there? Are they reliable? Are there clues to when and where it was filmed/photographed/recorded/written?

The media – and social media – are full of . . .

MISINFORMATION – saying or publishing something someone thinks is true but turns out not to be.

DISINFORMATION – the deliberate spreading of false information.

FAKE NEWS – 'news' that isn't real. It can be spread to suit someone's political agenda.

NEWSPAPERS

They are supposed to stick to a code of conduct that says they should not publish inaccurate, misleading or distorted information. But there is no requirement for them to present a balanced or unbiased view or account of events. When it comes to politics, most newspapers have a clear bias in favour of one of the main political parties. For example, the *Mail*, the *Telegraph*, the *Sun*, the *Express* and *The Times* are often biased for the Conservatives and against Labour, while the *Mirror* and to a lesser extent the *Guardian* are often biased for Labour.

Whilst newspapers should not be printing untruths, they can choose what they include and what they ignore. Newspapers also print opinion pieces and commentary, which are what they sound like – one person's opinion on something, not necessarily fact. Newspapers are supposed to make clear distinctions between factual reporting and opinion, but this does not always happen.

According to a survey done for my podcast, TV remains the most trusted form of media, followed by radio, then newspapers, with social media least trusted of all. But young people trust TV and radio less than older people.

WHAT CAN I DO PRACTICALLY?
The answer is **YOU DO WHATEVER YOU CAN.**
Here are some ideas to get you started . . .

WORK OUT WHAT YOU REALLY CARE ABOUT,
AND PUT IN THE TIME AND EFFORT TO
KNOW WHAT YOU ARE TALKING ABOUT.

ATTEND DEBATES. START
DEBATES. START A DEBATING
CLUB. STAND FOR THE
SCHOOL COUNCIL.

START OR SIGN PETITIONS.
PERSUADE YOUR FRIENDS TO
TAKE SERIOUS ISSUES SERIOUSLY.

IF THERE ARE CAUSES YOU BELIEVE IN, JOIN
LIKE-MINDED GROUPS, ATTEND MEETINGS,
GO ON MARCHES AND PROTESTS.

INFORM YOURSELF AND KEEP
INFORMING YOURSELF. READ
WIDELY. FOLLOW THE NEWS.

PRACTISE PUBLIC SPEAKING. EXPRESS YOUR
VIEWS. TRY TO PERSUADE PEOPLE TO COME
ROUND TO AND AGREE WITH YOUR VIEW.
PERSUADE WITHOUT JUDGEMENT (*SEE PAGE 128*).

HAVE IDEAS AND DON'T BE SCARED
TO RAISE THEM WITH OTHERS.

REACH OUT TO EXPERTS AND
PEOPLE WITH DIFFERENT VIEWS,
TO DEVELOP YOUR KNOWLEDGE . . .
KNOWLEDGE IS POWER!

IF YOU FEEL A PARTY REPRESENTS
YOUR VIEWS, JOIN IT. OR IF THERE
ARE CAMPAIGN GROUPS FIGHTING FOR
WHAT YOU BELIEVE IN, JOIN THEM TOO.
INFLUENCE HOW THEY OPERATE.

DON'T SEE IT AS A CHORE.
MAKE IT FUN.

WHAT IF I DON'T HAVE AN OPINION?

I'm sure you have opinions. Do you worry about climate change? Have you been upset and angered by war? Did you support or oppose teachers when they went on strike? Or is there something else you agree or disagree with? And if not yet, don't worry – follow the news, read widely, think about things, talk to people about what's happening in the country. You'll know what you think soon enough.

THE MAIN THING THAT GOT ME INTERESTED IN POLITICS WAS THAT I COULDN'T UNDERSTAND WHY SOME PEOPLE WERE REALLY RICH AND OTHERS WERE REALLY POOR.

WHAT IF I AM INTERESTED IN POLITICS BUT DON'T WANT TO BE A POLITICIAN?

No problem. Be a volunteer. Be a campaigner. Policy advisers, strategists, speechwriters, civil servants, organisers, designers, NGOs (non-governmental organisations) and charities . . . they are all part of politics. And there is local politics as well as national politics, and getting involved in your own area is often the best place to start.

WHAT IF I WANT TO BE A COUNCILLOR OR MP?

If you're 18 or over, go for it. It won't necessarily be easy though. You will need to be selected by a party, or stand as an independent, and when it comes to being selected to run as a parliamentary candidate, it can be a tough process, and you might not win. But far better to try than not, and even if you fail, you will learn something for the next time.

 WHAT CAN YOU DO NOW? CONSIDER STANDING FOR YOUR SCHOOL COUNCIL TO START PRACTISING THE SKILLS YOU'LL NEED. IF YOUR SCHOOL DOESN'T HAVE ONE, SPEAK TO A TEACHER ABOUT HOW TO START ONE.

WHAT MAKES A GOOD CANDIDATE?

You need to: know your own mind; know what you're talking about; know your local area inside out; be interested in and good with people; be a good communicator; be able to make decisions; lead a team and be a team player. Work hard. Really hard.

MY JOURNEY INTO POLITICS WAS VIA JOURNALISM. WHEN I WAS A POLITICAL REPORTER, I GOT TO KNOW LOTS OF POLITICIANS. I BECAME MORE AND MORE INTERESTED AND PASSIONATE ABOUT POLITICS, SO WHEN TONY BLAIR ASKED ME TO WORK FOR HIM, AND HELP HIM BECOME PM, I WENT FOR IT.

INTERVIEW WITH
JULIA GILLARD

Australia's first and, so far, only female
Prime Minister (2010–2013)

HAVE YOU ALWAYS LIVED IN AUSTRALIA?

I was born in Barry, South Wales, and moved
to Australia when I was five. My dad was
a psychiatric nurse and my mum worked in
a nursing home.

DID YOU ALWAYS WANT TO BE A POLITICIAN?

No. I was quite a shy child. I thought I might be
a teacher. It was the mother of a friend who urged
me to study law. That was good preparation for
politics, because it teaches you how to analyse
issues from every angle, and how to argue.

WHAT'S THE BEST THING ABOUT BEING A PM?

Being able to make decisions that can hopefully
make things better for people.

WHAT'S THE WORST THING?

The media exposure can be tough at times. Also,
you are not always in as much control as people
think because there are so many factors – and
people! – to consider.

DO YOU THINK MORE IS NEEDED TO HELP WOMEN IN POLITICS?

Politics has always been very male-dominated. In 2012, I gave a speech in Parliament that attacked the attitudes in politics that put women down or hold women back. It got a lot of attention because I think it spoke to the experience of women in politics everywhere. We have made a lot of progress, but there is a long way to go. There are around 200 countries in the world today, and fewer than two dozen with women leaders.

DID YOU RECEIVE A LOT OF ABUSE?

Yes, being in the spotlight can be difficult and unpleasant at times. However, there is no greater thrill than being able to represent people and make decisions that help them in their lives. When I look back on my career, I don't think of the barbs and insults. I think of all the things I did to help make life better for people.

WOULD YOU RECOMMEND POLITICS TO YOUNG PEOPLE?

Absolutely! It is more important than ever because there are so many difficult issues to deal with right now.

HOW DO I BUILD MY CONFIDENCE?

Fear of public speaking is one of the most common phobias in the world. You need to conquer it to go into politics. There are all sorts of ways you can learn to get over nerves, such as breathing deeply or practising in front of the mirror. I have a little tactic, rubbing my thumbs and forefingers together, which always works for me. But nothing beats doing public speaking, and then realising you did it well. It is important to know the difference between pressure, which can make us perform better, and stress. A bit of pressure is good. Stress is bad. Then pat yourself on the back when you've done something well. Confidence builds every time. And if it doesn't go to plan, don't worry – think of it as an opportunity to learn.

HOW DO I DEAL WITH HAVING DIFFERENT VIEWS TO MY FAMILY AND FRIENDS?

Just accept and respect the differences. But try not to fall out. I do a podcast with former Conservative minister Rory Stewart (*see pages 34–35*), and we have a motto: **DISAGREE AGREEABLY,** which means when we disagree, we do not attack each other personally, and we respect each other's views, even when our own view is different. Try to follow that.

I GOT A GREAT PIECE OF ADVICE FROM PUPIL ANNABELLE FOX DURING A SCHOOL VISIT. WHEN I ASKED HER HOW I SHOULD HANDLE SEVERAL HUNDRED BREXIT VOTERS ON A TV PROGRAMME I WAS SOON TO RECORD, SHE SAID: 'DON'T TRIM YOUR VIEWS, THEY WON'T RESPECT THAT. PERSUADE WITHOUT JUDGEMENT!'

WHAT DOES FREEDOM OF SPEECH MEAN?

Under the law, freedom of speech means you have the right to hold opinions and express them freely without government interference. There are limits though. You are not free to use threatening or abusive words in order to harass people, stir up violence or be racist, for example. All too often, people who claim their freedom of speech is limited simply mean they want the green light to be racist, sexist or critical of minorities.

DEBATING

So much of politics is about communication, and one of the top skills you need is being able to debate, which means discussing an issue by looking at opposite arguments. Speaking clearly and confidently is incredibly useful in everyday life too.

HOW DOES AN ORGANISED DEBATE WORK?

A speaker reads out a statement – called a motion – e.g. This House believes all schools should teach debating. The **proposer** gives their argument, which agrees with the motion. Then the **opposer** gives their argument, which disagrees with the motion. Other people may speak and there's a summing up by both sides. Then everyone present votes to decide who won the debate.

ALWAYS ATTACK THE IDEA, RATHER THAN THE PERSON.

'BY FAILING TO PREPARE, YOU ARE PREPARING TO FAIL.' THIS IS A FAMOUS QUOTE ATTRIBUTED TO AMERICAN STATESMAN BENJAMIN FRANKLIN, BUT THERE IS NO ACTUAL EVIDENCE HE SAID IT! IT IS WISE ADVICE, THOUGH!

TIPS FOR DEBATING

- When preparing, pick apart your own arguments by imagining what someone who disagrees with you would say, and work out what you would say back.

- Know your stuff: do the research and back up points with facts.

- Boil your main points down to a few words.

- Persuade with emotions – make people care by telling human stories, not just facts and figures (though these are important too).

- People like to be amused, so humour and wit can be a great way to get across serious points.

- Try to stay calm, even if the other person or team is trying to wind you up.

GET INVOLVED

The more debates you do, the more you will learn. Join your school council or debating team. If there isn't one, start one! It really is a good way to develop confidence, and to find out what motivates you.

IDEAS FOR DEBATES

Here are a few debate suggestions to get you going, with an argument for and an argument against. Let's start with things relevant to school life. Try to think of a few more arguments to add to the side of the debate you support.

This House believes . . .

EACH SCHOOL DAY SHOULD START WITH AN HOUR OF SPORT.

FOR: UK obesity crisis. Good for health and wellbeing.

AGAINST: More important things to learn. Some people hate sport.

THE VOTING AGE SHOULD BE LOWERED TO 16 ACROSS THE UK.

FOR: Will engage more people and energise them to get involved in politics.

AGAINST: Children don't know enough about politics.

IT CAN BE REALLY GOOD PRACTICE TO MAKE AN ARGUMENT FOR SOMETHING YOU DON'T ACTUALLY BELIEVE. THIS IS CALLED 'PLAYING DEVIL'S ADVOCATE.'

CHILDREN UNDER 14 SHOULD NOT HAVE SOCIAL-MEDIA ACCOUNTS.

FOR: Evidence that social-media addiction is causing mental-health problems.

AGAINST: Social media can be a great learning tool.

I WAS IN A SCHOOL RECENTLY WHERE WE HAD A VOTE ON THE SOCIAL-MEDIA QUESTION. TO MY SURPRISE, THE MOTION WON. ONE GIRL GAVE THIS REASON: 'I AM SEEING SO MUCH STUFF THAT I KNOW I SHOULDN'T.' IT WAS AN INTERESTING PERSPECTIVE.

MORE IDEAS FOR DEBATES

Now let's look at a few issues outside of school. Again, try to think of a few more arguments to add to the side of the debate you support.

This House believes . . .

THERE IS TOO MUCH IMMIGRATION INTO THE UK.

FOR: People coming to the UK put extra pressure on already stretched public services like hospitals.

AGAINST: There is a staffing crisis in the hospital and care sectors and we need more immigrants to fill those jobs.

WE SHOULD REPLACE THE KING WITH AN ELECTED PRESIDENT.

FOR: The monarchy is the pinnacle of a class system that is outdated and unfair.

AGAINST: The monarchy is popular and provides stability in a world of enormous change.

ALL TESTING ON ANIMALS FOR MEDICAL RESEARCH SHOULD BE BANNED.

FOR: Testing is cruel to the animals.

AGAINST: It can help develop new cures and treatments for killer illnesses and save many human lives.

THERE HAS NEVER BEEN A BETTER TIME TO BE A WOMAN.

FOR: There have been massive steps forward in women's equality.

AGAINST: Men often still earn more than women for doing the same job.

DON'T FORGET TO LISTEN — THIS IS A SKILL TOO. PAY ATTENTION TO WHAT THE OTHER PERSON IS SAYING AND SHOW YOU ARE LISTENING BY RESPONDING APPROPRIATELY. THIS WILL HELP YOU TO HAVE GOOD DISCUSSIONS WITH PEOPLE WHO HAVE DIFFERENT OPINIONS FROM YOURS.

CAMPAIGNING

Whether you're running to be Prime Minister, or a member of your school council, you'll need a campaign to help you win – but where do you start? Let me introduce you to **OST**, which I always use when working on campaigns to win elections or to make change . . .

O = OBJECTIVE

What do you want to achieve?

S = STRATEGY

How are you going to do it? In a word, a phrase, a sentence.

T = TACTICS

What does your strategy mean in practical terms?

Think of your campagain in that order. First O, then S, and only when you are clear about O and S, go into T.

Let's say you think your local skatepark or basketball court in the park is run down.

O = Get the local council to fund repairs.

S = Persuasion and protest.

T = You could petition, do press interviews for the local media, do your own blog, contact your local MP or a councillor, protest with a parent/guardian, try to get endorsement from the local community or a local celebrity!

Learn from similar campaigns happening in other parts of the country. Like Olivia Clarke, 21, who has won awards for her role successfully campaigning for free bus services for young people in Manchester.

COME UP WITH A SLOGAN. BUILD A TEAM. NEVER TIRE OF SAYING THE SAME THING. DON'T GIVE UP.

Above all, CARE. Here is one of my all-time favourite quotes, usually attributed to former US President Theodore Roosevelt: **'NOBODY CARES HOW MUCH YOU KNOW, UNTIL THEY KNOW HOW MUCH YOU CARE.'** Facts matter. But so do emotions. Care! Really care about the people and the world around you. Never say 'I'm not bothered.' Be bothered!

CAN ONE PERSON REALLY MAKE A DIFFERENCE?

Yes, they can! So whenever you hear someone say, 'There's no point getting involved because one person can't make a difference,' tell them they are wrong. Here are a few examples . . .

GRETA THUNBERG

One of the most famous climate campaigners in the world. Do you know why she was on her own when she first rose to prominence by staging a 'School strikes for the climate' protest outside the Swedish Parliament? Because it was raining and her friends decided not to go. She cared more. Also, Greta made herself an expert. She built a global profile and though the climate crisis is not over, she has made a difference by inspiring others to get involved.

GINA MARTIN

Gina fought and won a battle to get the law changed after young men took photos up her skirt – called upskirting. The police told her there was no law against it. There is now in England and Wales! She campaigned, and it happened.

MARCUS RASHFORD

Marcus is a famous footballer. But he's also someone who thinks it is wrong that some children go hungry, so he launched and won a campaign to make sure that children on free school meals still got food during the COVID-19 lockdowns. His petition received over one million signatures! This helped persuade the government to give £400 million to support families.

DAN LAWES, A YOUNG ACTIVIST FROM MANCHESTER, IS PASSIONATE ABOUT GIVING YOUNG PEOPLE FROM THE NORTH OF ENGLAND A VOICE. SINCE THE AGE OF 16, DAN HAS WORKED TIRELESSLY IN SCHOOLS AND COLLEGES. HE HELPED LEAD THE 'GIVE AN X' CAMPAIGN ON NATIONAL VOTER REGISTRATION DAY 2024, AND SET A SINGLE-DAY RECORD FOR THE NUMBER OF SIGN-UPS OF YOUNG PEOPLE AGED 18-34, AHEAD OF A UK LOCAL ELECTION.

METE COBAN, MBE.

DOES ANYTHING REALLY CHANGE?

Promise me you will never say, 'There is no point getting involved because nothing ever changes.' I've heard people say that all my life. I don't think there has ever been an era of so much change. Climate. Inequality. Conflict. AI will bring the next big wave of technological change – it will present huge opportunities, like better healthcare, but threats too, to millions of jobs that will be done by machines and transform the world of work. So, things change. The question we all face is whether we want to let the change wash over us or try to have our say and make our mark in whatever way we can, large or small.

IF YOU HAD SAID TO ME WHEN I WAS IN MY TEENS, THAT ONE DAY I WOULD HELP THE LABOUR PARTY WIN THREE GENERAL ELECTIONS, WORK FOR THE PRIME MINISTER IN DOWNING STREET, MEET NELSON MANDELA AND QUEEN ELIZABETH II, VISIT OVER 100 COUNTRIES AND BE INVOLVED IN HUGE ISSUES OF WAR AND PEACE, I WOULD NOT HAVE BELIEVED YOU. I DIDN'T PLAN ANY OF IT WHEN I WAS YOUNG. IT HAPPENED BECAUSE I WAS CURIOUS, PASSIONATE, HARD-WORKING . . . AND A BIT LUCKY. AND MAYBE YOU COULD DO STUFF TOO.

Thanks for reading the book – I hope you enjoyed it and now feel more empowered and confident when talking about politics. But if you don't know where to start, start by being interested and being informed. Read or watch the news; it can be very depressing, but it is important to know what is happening, good and bad, in your area, in the country, and abroad. Learn about big and difficult issues (such as pollution, poverty and homelessness). And never be afraid to ask questions. Always be curious, it's the best way to learn. Have a view. Take a stand. Learn how to argue, and be proud of knowing what you think, and saying so. Your voice matters every bit as much as anyone else's.

INDEX

Alastair Campbell is a writer, podcaster and strategist best known for his work as former Prime Minister Tony Blair's spokesperson and former Downing Street Director of Communications and Strategy. Still active in politics and campaigns in Britain and overseas, he now splits his time between writing, speaking, broadcasting, charity work and consultancy. He hosts the chart-topping podcast *The Rest is Politics* along with Rory Stewart. This is his 21st book, and is being published alongside *Why Politics Matters*, part of the Little Experts series for six- to nine-year-olds.